126 BULBS, CORMS AND TUBERS
IN COLOUR

WIM OUDSHOORN

126 BULBS, CORMS AND TUBERS IN COLOUR

Translated by Marian Powell

LUTTERWORTH PRESS • GUILDFORD AND LONDON

Drawings: Marjolein Bastin

Photographs: Frits Boldingh, Aerdenhout; Centraal Bloembollen Comite, Hillegom; C. H. v. Helvoort, Amersfoort; Jan den Hengst, Aarlanderveen; Wim Oudshoorn, Oegstgeest; Anton v. Overveld, Rijswijk; G. Papendrecht, Lisse; Horticultural Testing Station, Aalsmeer; Harry Smith, Westcliffe on Sea; Fa. Tubergen, Haarlem; Henk Zevenbergen, Rijswijk.

First published in Great Britain in 1974

ISBN 0 7188 2124 6

Filmset by Keyspools Ltd., Golborne, Lancs.

Printed in the Netherlands

CONTENTS

126 BULBS, CORMS AND TUBERS IN COLOUR

You would be well advised to give a wide meaning to the title of this book, as is, in fact, indicated by the sub-title.

One generally speaks of bulbs and tubers but bear in mind that this phrase also includes plants grown from rhizomes, etc.

In any case it is of little importance to you, the reader, how the various groups of plants are divided; on the other hand you will get on much better if you have some knowledge of the main points. So, here we go . . . join me in a short botany lesson.

The herbaceous plants we use in our gardens are sometimes divided into perennials, annuals and biennials, bulbous and tuberous plants. Perennials are herbaceous growths which are hardy, that is, plants which come up every spring, flower and form seeds, and then die down late in the autumn, but survive underground in their roots. Among perennials are such well-known plants as Michaelmas daisies, lupins, peonies and marguerites.

Annuals are also herbaceous plants. They increase by means of their seed. Within one calendar year the seed germinates, a plant is formed, flowers, produces seed and dies (for instance, marigold, antirrhinum, petunia, African marigold).

Biennials form mostly roots and leaves within the first year. They hibernate in winter and in the second year the stem develops and flowers are formed. After flowering they die (for instance honesty, hollyhock).

Bulbous and tuberous plants occupy an entirely different place. They store food in their underground parts, often in the form of food. Bulbs and tubers may therefore be regarded as store rooms.

A bulb consists of a short stem, the basal plate, and thick, fleshy leaves (the scales). In other words, a bulb is really a stem with leaves. On top of the basal plate we find the terminal bud, which develops into the part of the plant which is above ground. In the axillae of the scales grow the axillary buds, which develop into young bulbs. These young bulbs are often used for propagation. When the young growth of a tulip (the terminal bud) emerges from the soil in spring, it does so at the expense of the food stored in the scales.

Meanwhile roots have formed, and continue to form. The

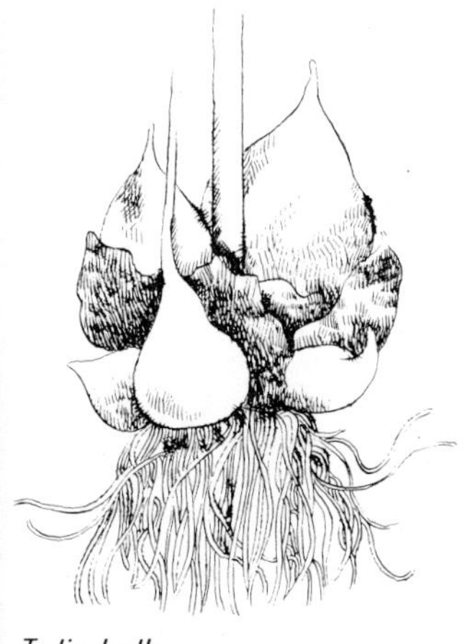

*Tulip bulb
with progeny*

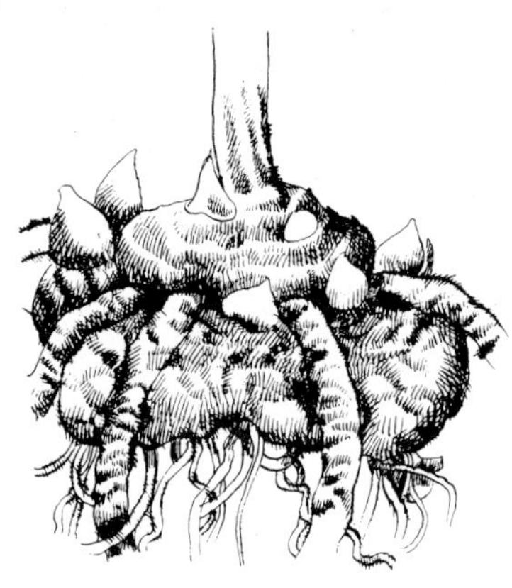

*Old and new
gladiolus corms*

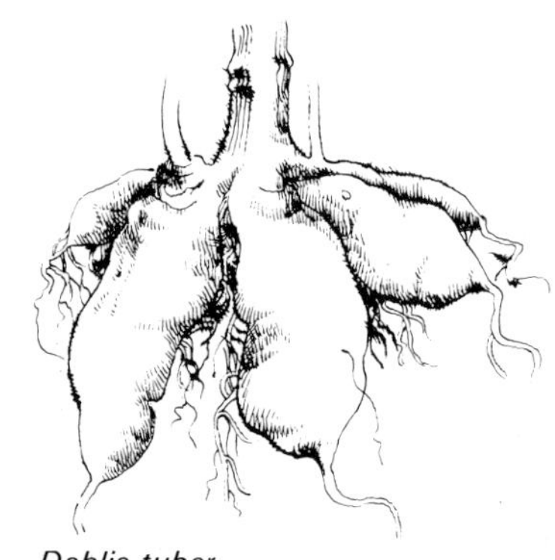

Dahlia tuber

plant is therefore able to take up water and nourishment through its roots. The foliage also absorbs nourishment, and sugar and starch are formed. A 'surplus' of food is created in the plant, which is transported to the bulb, enabling the main bud and the axillary buds to develop into new bulbs.

In the case of the tulip, the entire bulb is used up during one growing season. Of the old bulb, planted in November, practically nothing remains when the plants are cleared in June—July.

The bulbs of the hyacinth and the daffodil, on the other hand, remain intact for several years. Not the entire bulb is emptied, only the outer scales, while new ones are continuously being formed from the centre. The young bulbs developed from the axillary buds are initially attached to the mother bulb at its basal plate.

Corms, too, are stores of reserve food. In the case of a corm this food is not stored in leaves, but in the stem. Corms are found, amongst others, in the gladiolus and the crocus. Young corms (or cormlets) develop on top of the old ones. The overground parts of both the crocus and gladiolus develop from a number of buds growing on the upper part of the corm. Surplus food formed during growth is transported to the lower part of the young stems, which thus develop into young corms. Tubers are another method by which plants store food; in this case they may either be swollen underground stems, as in cyclamen, or swollen roots, e.g. dahlias. When the tuber is a swollen stem it is best differentiated from a corm by the fact that it has no membraneous coat.

Bulbous, cormous and tuberous plants are found all over the world.

Many lilies are natives of China and Japan. One eremurus species (Foxtail lily) is found in the Himalayas.

Gladioli and freesias originate in South Africa. In South America, too, bulbous-type plants are found growing wild; for instance the dahlia grows naturally in Mexico. In the western states of the U.S.A. one of the native bulbous plants is the camassia. In Europe also, a number are found growing wild, for instance a species of Star of Bethlehem (Ornithogalum umbellatum) and Ransoms (Allium ursinum). Is it not amazing that all these plants, originating in so many different parts of the world, are grown successfully over here? After all, both soil and climate in their country of origin are often quite different.

THE HISTORY OF BULB GROWING IN BRITAIN

Bulbs have been grown in Britain for a very long time, but they have always been rather more popular in Holland, where they have been grown for even longer. It is not possible to determine when they were first used there, but what is certain is that they were imported from Southern and South-eastern Europe as early as the Middle Ages.

At that time bulbous plants were not, however, grown purely for their decorative effect, either in Britain or Holland. They were mostly grown in monastery gardens, since some of them were deemed to have medicinal properties.

One of the great Dutch herbalists, Rembert Dodens (1517–1585), described the tulip in his *Cruydtboek* (Herbal). From his description it may be deduced that great importance was attached to the curative and edible qualities of plants. The following is an extract from the book:

'Earth, Power and Effect. The properties of the Tulipa have not yet been investigated and as far as we know have never yet been described.'

And in the Addendum:

'Like the onion, bulbs of the tulip may be used in a salad with oil and vinegar, for they taste good or at least are not nauseous.'

This was certainly borne out in Holland in the famine winter of 1944–1945 when the Dutch were forced to eat tulip bulbs. Not 'nauseous', but certainly not very nice; however, there is no accounting for taste.

In Britain Richard Hakluyt, a naval historian, wrote in 1582 that:

'Within these four years there have been brought into England from Vienna in Austria divers kinds of flowers called tulipes, and these and others procured thither a little before Constantinople by an excellent man called M. Carolus Clusius.'

It was Carolus Clusius, the first Professor of Botany in Leyden, who started the cultivation of bulbs in Holland. He received tulip bulbs and/or seeds from a certain Ghiselin de Busbecq, who was the Austrian emperor's ambassador to Turkey. At that time the tulip was already held in high esteem among Turks and Persians, and celebrations were held during its flowering season. It is certain that the Turks had already hybridised many varieties and species, and had thus created all sorts of new forms and strains.

We see, therefore, that the tulip, one of the most popular and well-known of bulbs, was cultivated in Europe by the 16th century, as was the hyacinth.

Clusius possessed a considerable collection of bulbous plants. Collectors began to exchange species and soon afterwards a keen trade in bulbs began.

It became fashionable to grow bulbs, and increasingly high prices were paid for them. This led to excesses. Between 1634 and 1637 Holland was held in the grip of the so-called Tulip Mania. Excessive prices were paid for a single bulb. They reached such levels that bulbs began to be sold per perit — a weight used by goldsmiths. One perit is the equivalent of 1/20th gram! Prices rose to 2000, 3000 and even 4000 Dutch florins (one florin is approximately 16p) for a single bulb. The so-called 'broken' varieties, in particular, fetched high prices. ('Broken' tulips are bi-coloured; for instance a red tulip with irregular white feathering).

It goes without saying that this unhealthy trade had to be stopped. A great deal of swindling went on. There were many sales the only aim of which was to force up prices still further.

In 1637 the bubble burst. Prices fell with alarming speed and in the end the Dutch States General laid down rules for the transactions already effected. In spite of, or perhaps because of, this Tulip Mania, the cultivation of bulbs became permanently established in Holland (initially in and around Haarlem).

Approximately a century later a similar situation arose in connection with hyacinths. Again ridiculous prices were paid. The authorities issued grave warnings, and this time the speculative trade did not attain quite such proportions. Nevertheless, the hyacinth retained its popularity for a long time. In the 18th century any mention of bulbs referred to hyacinth bulbs. New cultivars were produced and double-flowered kinds were grown, which have long since disappeared from the scene.

In his book *The Trade in Bulbs*, the Dutch expert Dr. Verhage states that in 1870 approximately 400 hectares were planted with bulbs. By 1900 this had grown to 1500 hectares. Between 1900 and 1932 the area regularly increased. At that time the depression claimed its toll. Towards the end of the second world war the total area under bulb cultivation probably shrank to under 4000 hectares, but after the war bulb-growing recovered fairly rapidly.

Nowadays bulb-culture is again of great importance. The area under cultivation has reached hitherto unknown proportions, and export figures do not lie.

BULB GROWING IN BRITAIN

Traditionally, Britain is an importer of flower bulbs; at present it imports about £5½m. each year, mostly from the Netherlands. However, Britain is not without its own bulb growers, in fact it has a well-established and flourishing industry. According to a census, carried out by the Ministry of Agriculture, Fisheries and Food in June 1973, some 17,626 acres are given over to bulb growing and the latest figures for the main bulk crops are as follows:

Narcissus	10,727 acres (1972)
Tulips	3,664 acres (1972)
Gladiolus	921 acres (1973)
Iris	342 acres (1973)

Although Anemones are not recorded by census, it is estimated that there are about 400 acres grown. The Narcissus acreage is greater than that in any other country and might well be greater than the rest of the world put together.

The British bulb industry is located mainly in two regions:

(a) *Eastern England* (from the Humber to Norfolk) which accounts for some 80 per cent of all outdoor acreage. Here, the most concentrated area is south Lincolnshire (Holland), its rich alluvial soils accounting for 58 per cent of the national acreage.

(b) *South West England* which accounts for 12 per cent of the national acreage. Most of this is in the extreme west of Cornwall and the Isles of Scilly, but there is a small acreage in the Tamar valley.

The remaining 8 per cent is scattered throughout the country.

Recently, Britain has even started to export both flowers and bulbs. This trade effectively began in 1970 when flowers and bulbs to the value of £64,000 were exported. By 1973 this figure had risen to over £300,000 and the industry shows every sign of continuing to expand. Our exports go mainly to Europe where the chief importers are first, Holland, and second, West Germany.

PROPAGATION

To private garden owners the methods of propagation may be of little importance. Nevertheless, it is useful and interesting to devote a few lines to this subject, particularly as the layman often has an entirely inaccurate idea of how it is done.

In the first place we should mention generic propagation. Miscellaneous plants are often grown from seed, for instance, to name only a few: anemone, eranthis (winter aconite), eremurus (Foxtail lily), brodiaea, chionodoxa (Glory of the Snow), scilla and puschkinia.

In principle, of course, all bulbous and cormous plants can be grown from seed, but if one sows, for instance, a particular yellow tulip or a blue hyacinth, the result may not breed true. All sorts of colours and shapes may result. Often we find not a single flower identical to the plant from which the seed was won. Moreover, it may be several years before flowering bulbs are produced from seed.

Tulips, gladioli, crocuses, etc., can also be propagated by means of division. We might say that they multiply themselves.

Tulip bulbs are annual. The bulbs we plant in November have disappeared entirely when the plants are lifted in the following year. Instead we find not only a large new bulb, but also a number of smaller ones.

The bulb of the daffodil, however, lasts for several seasons. New bulbs develop by the side of the old one, constantly adding new scales. Eventually the old bulb 'bursts from its jacket' and the young bulbs grow detached from the parent bulb, the lower part at first remaining attached. We often see daffodils with these offspring; the outer ones are called offsets. These eventually separate from the parent bulb and are cultivated for subsequent propagation.

Gladioli and crocuses are propagated in a slightly different manner. They have an annual corm. One or more young corms develop on top of the old one which withers away; the newly-formed corms are then re-planted. Occasionally, as in the case of gladioli and freesias, so-called 'spawn' is formed; tiny cormlets growing on the parent corm.

In the case of tulips, daffodils, crocuses and gladioli we might therefore speak of natural propagation. It should be

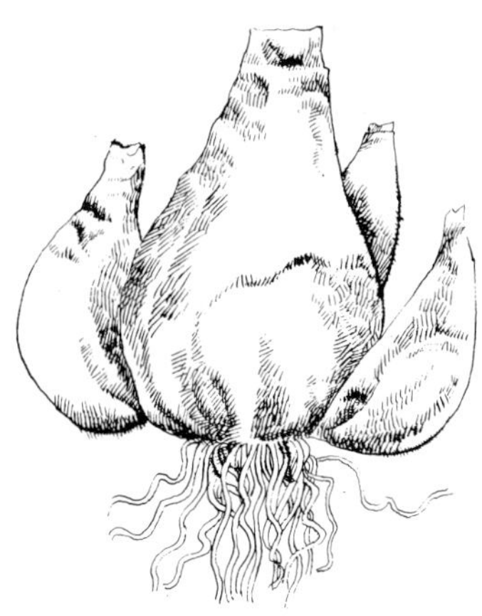

*Narcissus bulb
with offsets*

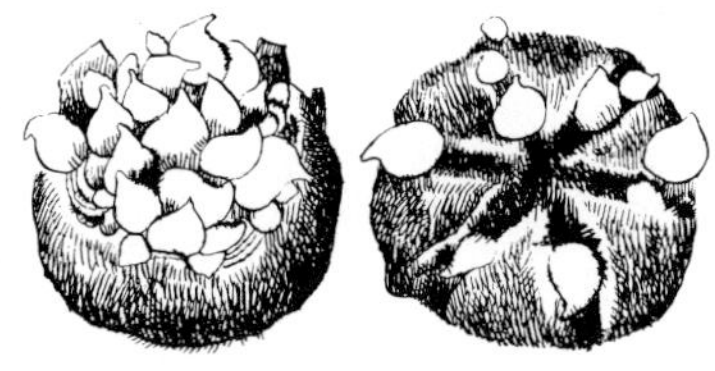

*Left, a hollowed,
right, a notched
hyacinth bulb*

mentioned that bulb-growers can encourage the development of many young bulbs by various methods (in the case of tulips, for instance, by regulating the temperature during the dormant period).

A special method of propagation is used in the case of hyacinths. Growers call this method 'following' or 'cutting', meaning the removal or notching of the basal plate. By this method a large number of small young bulbs are produced, which may develop into marketable bulbs within two or three years.

This may seem a simple operation, but great expertise is required to do the job properly. The hollowed or notched bulbs must, moreover, be kept at certain temperatures and high levels of humidity for several weeks before they can be planted.

Dahlias, finally, are usually propagated by soft cuttings. In February—March the tubers are placed in moist peat in the greenhouse. Shoots appear, which are cut off. These shoots are set in compost in boxes or pots and form roots, and the young plants are put out in the open in late May, when all fear of frost is past.

HOW ARE NEW VARIETIES CREATED?

Catalogues constantly draw attention to new tulips, daffodils and narcissi, dahlia-cultivars, crocuses, etc. These new products may have different colours, be more vigorous, flower earlier or have other improved characteristics.

The interested layman will no doubt have wondered at times how all these new cultivars are created. There are a number of firms in Britain who specialise in crossing various types and varieties in order to produce new forms with improved properties. The following fictitious case may serve as an example:

A tall, yellow, late-flowering tulip, perfect in shape and very suitable for cutting, may not be very satisfactory for growing in the garden because its stem is too long and limp, and because it flowers rather late. It is desirable to keep the shape and colour, while getting rid of the less attractive characteristics, such as the long stem and the late flowering period. In other words, an early-flowering, low-growing, well-shaped yellow tulip is sought, which is more suitable for use in the garden.

An early-flowering, short-stemmed *white* tulip of average shape is available. By crossing the two varieties it is possible that one of the many seeds will produce a bulb with characteristics which approximate to the desired result. Thus the aim will have been achieved: a new cultivar has been created.

The above puts the case very simply, in fact far *too* simply. It takes a profound knowledge of the theory of heredity and great expertise to achieve anything in this field. And even then good results are obtained only after many years of perseverance.

Some plants at times produce mutants, which the trade calls 'sports'. A mutant is a sudden, inheritable divergence in a plant's characteristics. A batch of red tulip bulbs may suddenly produce one with a yellow flower. All other properties are the same, only the colour differs. This yellow tulip is kept apart when the bulbs are lifted and is cultivated separately. It is not only the colour which may change; other properties, too, may mutate. For instance, flowering may take place earlier or later; the plant may be more (or less) vigorous; it may grow taller or produce a larger number of petals (become double-flowered). If the change is an improvement, the bulbs are of course carefully segregated and grown separately.

Such mutants occur particularly among tulips and dahlias. It is not yet entirely clear how these mutants are created. It is possible that cosmic radiation plays a part, but this does not explain why some plants mutate often, while others do so rarely or never.

Nowadays it is possible to produce mutants artificially by means of radiation.

THE NAMING OF BULBOUS AND TUBEROUS PLANTS

Every plant has a botanical name in accordance with the system of binary nomenclature. We owe this system, in which the name of the plant is composed of two parts, a generic name and one which indicates the species, to Carolus Linnaeus (1707–1778). These scientific names are essential for the maintenance of international contacts between botanists and horticulturalists.

Many plants have a common name as well, but this may lead to confusion. To give you an example: there is a bulbous plant called 'Star of Bethlehem' of which the botanical name is Ornithogalum umbellatum. But there is also a well-known pot plant (Campanula isophylla) called 'Star of Bethlehem'. The two plants have nothing in common apart from the fact that they both bear white flowers. They are not related in any way and indeed belong to two entirely different families.

Most bulbous and tuberous plants belong to the Order of Lilliflorae. As the name implies, plants belonging to this Order have flowers resembling the lily. The Order consists of three families, namely the liliaceae, the amaryllidaceae and the iridaceae.

To the liliaceae belong, among others, the lily, the tulip, the hyacinth and the ornithogalum (Star of Bethlehem). Among the amaryllidaceae we count, for instance, the narcissus, the snowdrop and the ixiolirion. Apart from the iris, the crocus, the gladiolus and the ixia belong to the iridaceae.

Each plant name begins with the generic name, which is always written with a capital letter, e.g. Tulipa, Narcissus, Dahlia and Freesia. The specific name is always written with a small first letter. This is the name which describes the name further, which is necessary, since there are genera consisting of as many as 100 species.

Sometimes the specific name indicates certain characteristics. Occasionally the country of origin or the place where the plant was found occurs in the name. Names of persons, too, are often included in specific names. The following are some examples:

Colchicum autumnale (=autumn-flowering)
Anemone blanda (=charming)
Eranthis hyemalis (=winter-flowering)

Sparaxis tricolor (= three-coloured)
Cyclamen europaeum (= originating in Europe)
Sprekelia formosissima (= the most beautiful)
Lilium candidum (= pure white)
Corydalus solida (= firm)
Lilium henryi (= after its discoverer, Dr. Henry)
Galanthus nivalis (= snow-white)

Many plants which originally grew wild have been crossed to achieve finer and better forms. Often it is no longer possible to establish which species have played a part in the crossing process; in that case we speak of hybrids. The word 'hybrid' is usually omitted. In the course of many years of cultivation numerous cultivars have appeared; there are, for instance, thousands of tulip cultivars. These have no botanic name, only fancy names. These are written with a capital letter and are placed in parentheses.

Some examples:
Tulipa 'Electra'
Narcissus 'Golden Harvest'
Hyacinthus 'City of Haarlem'
Crocus 'Remembrance'
Iris reticulata 'Cantab'
Scilla sibirica 'Spring Beauty'
Muscari botryoides 'Album'

HOW TO USE BULBOUS AND TUBEROUS PLANTS

The layman may use these plants in many different ways.

In the garden they may be planted in borders, beds or rock gardens. Many species are, moreover, suitable for underplanting or for naturalising in grass. A few species, such as eremurus (Foxtail lily) and Fritillaria imperialis (Crown Imperial) may, in fact, be used as specimen plants. Unlike trees and shrubs, however, they can only serve in this way for a limited period. In window-boxes, too, a fine effect may be achieved with bulbs and tubers.

Indoor cultivation is an entirely different form of use.

Anemones of the blanda species look fine when allowed to grow in wild profusion.

Tulips, hyacinths, daffodils and narcissi, for example, can be brought to flower in the living room. This indoor cultivation is briefly described in Table 7 at the end of this book.

More and more plant-lovers nowadays reserve part of their garden for flowers for cutting. Numerous bulbous and tuberous plants are suitable for this purpose. The following is a list of plants suitable for different purposes:

A. *For planting in borders:* tulips, daffodils, narcissi, various species of allium, lilies, iris, dahlia, gladioli, camassia, acidanthera, galtonia, tigridia (Tiger flower).

B. *For rock gardens:* crocus, erythronium (Dog's-tooth violet), Iris reticulata, I. danfordiae, Oxalis adenophylla, species tulips, some allium species, some species narcissi, Fritillaria imperialis (Crown Imperial).

C. *For planting in beds:* hyacinth, single and double early tulips, muscari (Grape hyacinth), dwarf dahlia, canna and tuberous begonia.

D. *Underplanting (naturalisation):* Anemone blanda, chionodoxa (Glory of the snow), scilla (Squill), eranthis (winter aconite), fritillaria (Guinea-hen flower), corydalis.

E. *For planting in lawns:* crocus, galanthus (snowdrop), daffodils, leucojum (snowflakes), etc.

BUYING BULBS AND TUBERS

The question arises, where to buy the required bulbs? We should like to emphasise that the purchase of these products is very much a matter of trust. However fine a bulb may appear, there is always the chance that there is something wrong with it. These 'hidden defects' are difficult or even impossible to detect. It is therefore advisable to go to a specialist. If your garden is maintained more or less regularly by a garden contractor, you would do well to order from him.

Bulbous plants provide plenty of colour in the border early in the year.

Another possibility is to order the bulbs from one of the firms specialising in retail sales. Most of these firms have an excellent reputation. They can in any case only maintain themselves by supplying a good product. In addition there are many shops dealing in seed, garden requirements, etc., where good bulbs may also be obtained. Gardening centres, too, often have a good assortment. Buying bulbs in large, apparently cheap quantities may lead to disappointment. Far be it for us to imply that everything sold under such conditions is rubbish, but experience has shown that inferior products sometimes reach the consumer via the market trade. Purchasing bulbs and tubers in department stores has another disadvantage. The sales staff in these places is not always very knowledgeable. Often the packing is very attractive (sometimes even misleading), but the quality is not always in keeping.

In this connection we should like to point out that bulbs (e.g. tulips) with a torn skin, or even without a skin, are not necessarily of bad quality. Some cultivars have a very loose-fitting 'tunic'. However, such bulbs must be treated with extra care, as damage to the scales may lead to the occurrence of various kinds of fungus. Bulbs which already betray the presence of disease or insect parasites (aphides) should never be accepted. In general only bulbs of so-called marketable size (indicated by size number) are offered for sale. When discussing the various plants this size will often be referred to; it indicates the circumference in centimetres at the widest part of the bulb. Marketable sizes will in normal circumstances produce flowers. It is advisable to buy the bulbs or have them sent just before you intend to plant them.

Large firms keep their various products at the most favourable temperatures. This points to another disadvantage of buying from markets or stores, where bulbs may be lying for weeks in various temperatures and widely fluctuating levels of humidity. When you get the bulbs you should therefore plant them immediately. Treat them with the greatest possible care and make sure they are not bruised. Bulbs are living organisms and should be treated as such. After all, in some species (tulips and hyacinths among others) the flowers are already present within the bulbs when you plant them.

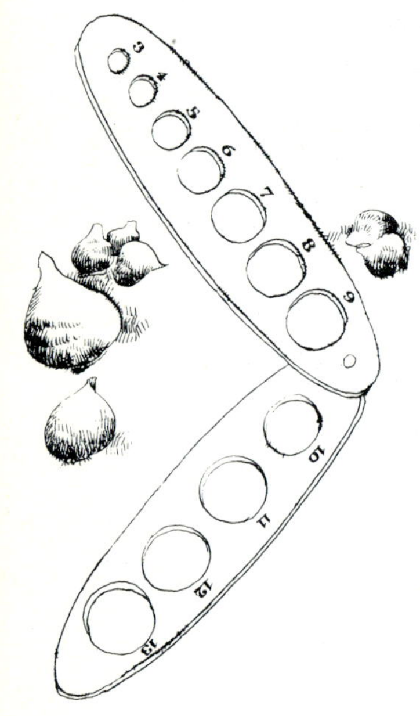

Bulb gauge

Dahlias, as well as being good for cutting, are also excellent border plants.

SOIL AND MANURING

In talking about soil and manuring in connection with bulbs and tubers, we should distinguish between their cultivation and their use in the garden.

The bulb-grower's aim is to achieve maximum production from the bulbs he has planted. For example, when the bulb-grower plants a miscellaneous lot of tulips, he expects the bulbs to double in number. A miscellaneous lot is one containing both large (e.g. size 13) bulbs as well as small ones (sizes 5 and 6). When he plants 1 cwt. (50 kg) he hopes to harvest 2 cwt. (100 kg) and this is well within the bounds of possibility. However, results depend on the species, growing conditions, the condition of the bulbs as well as of the soil and the way it has been manured.

It goes without saying that a great deal of attention is paid to the soil and its improvement and especially to manuring. Some bulbous plants, such as hyacinths, are very particular as regards soil. Cultivation is, in fact, successful only in coarse sandy soil containing only a small quantity of humus (rotted vegetable and animal matter) and clay particles. Not every bulb has such exact requirements: the tulip, for instance, will flourish in light clay soil as well as in sandy soil.

These requirements are of little importance to private gardeners. To them the main thing is to plant healthy bulbs which flower abundantly. Propagation is of minor interest. Most bulbs do well even in soil which is never manured.

When making a border which is to contain bulbous plants as well as others, rotted stable manure or garden compost is dug in, possibly after previous soil improvement. Dried cow dung is also excellent. Early in spring (February—March) an artificial compound fertiliser may be applied; this is especially desirable if you want to use the bulbs more than once. This fertiliser is best applied in dry weather and before the tips of the bulbs separate. It works best if there is rain after the fertiliser has been scattered. Care should be taken regarding the quantity used — an application of $\frac{3}{4}$ ounce per square yard is sufficient. This powder fertiliser is easily scattered and need not be dug in.

Whenever a plant has specific requirements this will be mentioned under its particular heading. It happens, for instance, that bulbous plants are intolerant of fresh stable manure. This applies to fritillaria (Crown Imperial and Guinea-hen flower) and leucojum (Snowflakes)

The Keukenhof in Holland is well worth a visit.

PLANTING

Most bulbs are planted in autumn, October and November being most suitable. Very early planting has the disadvantage that the bulbs come up too soon, which means that the young leaves of the developing plant may be damaged by frost. Too late planting delays flowering and sometimes prevents good development.

Another group of bulbs and tubers is planted in spring. These are often plants originating in warm countries: they flower in summer or late summer. Before planting the soil should be dug to a depth of 30 cm (12 in.).

When discussing the various products the depth at which they should be planted is always stated in centimetres (inches). This depth depends on various circumstances. Time of planting, size, and type of soil all play a part.

Sometimes it is difficult to see which is the top and which the bottom of a bulb. This is, for instance, the case with the anemone, so great care must be taken.

Be sure to plant the bulbs and tubers upright. They should be carefully covered with soil. If you want to plant a large group of bulbs it is advisable to make a pit of the desired depth. After having made sure that the subsoil has been loosened, the surface of the pit should be levelled. The bulbs are then planted at the desired distance apart and the soil which was removed is returned.

Another method for planting small lots (see lower two photographs p. 25) is as follows:

Place the bulbs *in situ* on top of the soil at the desired distance from each other and plant them one by one by hand or with a trowel. With this method the chance that one bulbs is planted deeper than another is of course greater. Small bulbs are sometimes planted by making a hole in the ground with a dibble, putting the bulb in and covering it with soil.

CARE AND STORAGE

As far as care in growing is concerned, bulbous and tuberous plants are not really very exacting. Generally

Bulbs, in this case tulips, may be planted in various ways.

speaking they need not be watered. Of course there are exceptions to this rule; for instance, when rooted dahlia cuttings are planted in late May, it may be necessary to give them some water in dry periods. Bulbs, however, are generally planted in autumn. This means that root-forming takes place during the winter, so that by the time spring arrives the plants usually have a considerable root system, capable of drawing nourishment and water from the soil. It is advisable to remove dead flowers, not only because they look unsightly, but also because seed formation exhausts the plants. We should therefore certainly advise you to remove dead flowers not only from plants which are kept *in situ*, but also from those which are lifted for storage.

In practice, however, bulbs (tulip, hyacinth, etc.) are usually lifted immediately after flowering. Often annuals are planted in the vacated spaces. If you want to keep the bulbs, they should be clamped in a corner of the garden together with their still-green parts.

For this purpose they are put in trenches at the same depth at which they were originally planted, and covered with soil. Once the top growth has died back, the bulbs can be lifted, cleaned, dried and stored, to be used again in the autumn.

Storage is quite difficult. Books dealing with the actual cultivation of bulbs indicate different and widely varying maximum temperature for the various bulbs. We find varying storage temperatures even for different tulip cultivars. Commercial bulb sheds nowadays are divided into 'temperature cells', in which widely varying temperatures may be maintained. In fact, in the course of storage, the bulbs are subjected to successive changes in temperature.

Of course, the private gardener cannot hope to achieve these conditions even by approximation, but one requirement can and must be met: the bulbs should be kept dry. This means that they must be absolutely dry before being put in their temporary store. As regards the temperature during storage we are greatly dependent on the weather. For hyacinths the temperature should be between 20 and 25° C (68–77° F). Tulips, too, are preferably kept fairly warm, 23–25° C (73–77° F).

Far be it for us to suggest that it is useless to store bulbs during the summer, but it must be said that in general the quality suffers. For that reason it is best to plant second-year tulips, etc. in a special corner reserved for cut flowers. Of the chief products (tulip, daffodil, narcissus and hyacinth), the narcissus is most suitable for storage — the bulbs may

By planting in large groups a solid effect is achieved.

even be kept outdoors (provided they are under cover).

As a rule, however, daffodil bulbs are left in the ground and this works for several years. If you want to be certain to have the best quality each year, you would undoubtedly do best each year to buy new bulbs from a reputable source. But if you like to experiment — what is to stop you?

Summer-flowering products, such as dahlia, begonia, gladiolus and so on are an entirely different matter. Gladioli are difficult to keep for an amateur; it is important to dry them very rapidly. Dahlia tubers and begonia corms, however, can be stored with success. The rule for these is: store in a dry, cool, but absolutely frost-free place. After they have been dried, they are best kept in peat fibre in a cellar.

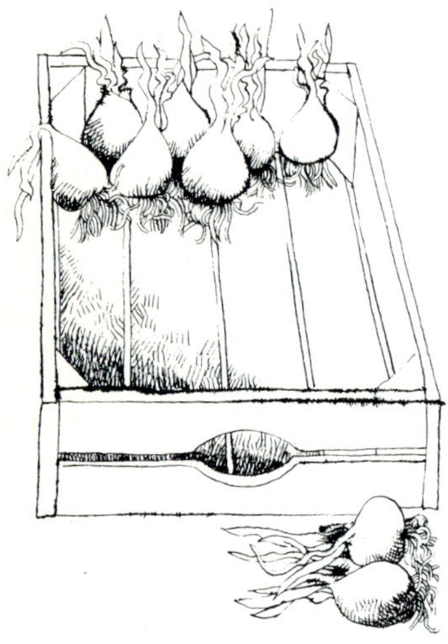

DISEASES AND DAMAGE

Bulbs and tubers, too, may be subject to insect and vegetable parasites. The number of different parasites is enormous. Bulky books have been written on this subject alone. Numerous officials of the Agricultural Development Advisory Service, the Plant Pathology Laboratory at Harpenden, Herts., Rosewarne Exp. Station, Cornwall, and Kirton Exp. Station, Boston, Lincs., are daily occupied with advising growers and with inspecting batches of bulbs. In the various laboratories university graduates and botanical analysts are trying to solve the problems caused by these parasites. Every year dozens of new pest controls are tested in the various research centres. It is beyond the scope of this book to dwell on this subject.

We shall therefore proceed from the standpoint that the grower, aided by scientific research and information, does everything possible to supply a first-class product. This can in any case only be to his own advantage. Just consider the huge interests involved in the export of bulbs.

The fact that it is not easy to control all insects and vegetable parasites is evident from the multitude of diseases which may occur in the various plants. Tulips, for instance, are subject to no fewer than eight vegetable parasites (moulds and bacteria) and several insect pests.

Various rhododendrons and azaleas flower at the same time as bulbous plants — here, for instance, with scilla.

What precautions should be take in the garden? In the first place it is not advisable to plant certain bulbs (e.g. tulips) in the same place in consecutive years, for the soil may retain certain fungus diseases which cause root rot and basal rot. Newly planted bulbs may be affected. The diseases may be prevented from infecting the bulbs by treating them before planting with a dip in a solution of the systemic fungicide benomyl (sold at Benlate), according to the maker's instructions. This fungicide is obtainable in small packs from garden shops. It is advisable to apply it in the case of other bulbs as well, e.g. iris, crocus, fritillaria and grape hyacinth, as well as the ordinary hyacinth. Benomyl is also very useful for controlling various fungal diseases which infect the top growth of bulbs, or which appear during storage. Application may be made as a pre-storage dip or as a spray to the top growth. It is not poisonous.

Aphides may also occur on various plants in the garden. There are various chemicals on the market which will control these pests, but be careful in their use. In fact, it is preferable not to use them at all.

BULBOUS PLANTS ATTRACTIVE TO BEES AND OTHER INSECTS

A flower, of whatever kind, is the finest part of a plant. The petals are brilliantly coloured in order to attract insects, for it is these which provide one of the methods by which pollination takes place, enabling the plant to produce seed. Thus the continued existence of a species is ensured.

But man knows better: flowers are there to captivate our eyes; seed formation is often not desirable, for division is the most generally used method of propagation. The less chance the plant has to form seed, the bigger and more numerous the bulbs will grow.

But to us garden-lovers the case is quite different. We are not interested in maximal propagation by division. We are garden-lovers and therefore admire living nature, that is, everything that nature has to offer, including the honey bees

A feast of colour in the snow.

and bumble-bees and all the other insects frequenting the flowers in our garden.

The grape hyacinth is an exceptionally fine flower and we enjoy its appearance. But our enjoyment may be intensified when we see the honey-bees working the flowers. The fact that the plant's flowering period will be slightly curtailed must be accepted into the bargain. When we see the bees move from one blossom to another with a passion that seems almost unreal, we can hardly begrudge them this activity. Nor would we want to.

The number of bulbous and tuberous plants that are attractive to honey-bees because of their nectar or pollen content is relatively small. In spring the crocus is most welcome to the bees, as it produces large quantities of pollen. The snowdrop, too, can provide pollen and nectar, but it flowers so early that it is of little or no interest to insects. A great deal of pollen is collected from the dahlia (at least from the single-flowered forms). We should also include the following: allium, chionodoxa, hyacinthus, leucojum, puschkinia and scilla.

Acidanthera bicolor 'Murielae'

Allium giganteum

ACIDANTHERA BICOLOR

Apart, of course, from gladioli, dahlias and tuberous begonias, summer-flowering bulbs are not very popular among garden owners. Wrongly so, for there are numerous fine species. One of these is the acidanthera, sometimes called the Abyssinian gladiolus.

This name immediately betrays two facts, namely the plant's relationship to the well-known gladiolus, and the country of origin: Abyssinia, present-day Ethiopia. The form 'Murielae' is the best to grow.

The plant, which flowers in August and September, is very effective in the border when used in groups of about ten among perennials. It is fragrant.

We plant the bulbs in late April at a depth of about 7 cm (3 in.). They should be lifted in October and stored frost-free during the winter.

ALLIUM GIGANTEUM

The genus Allium embraces numerous species. It is of great economical importance, for there are many edible forms, such as the common onion (A. cepa), the leek (A. porrum) and the shallot (A. ascalonicum).

The 'giant onion', A. giganteum, is a particularly fine species, originating in the Himalayas. It has a large globular inflorescence in June, consisting of an umbel of reddish-purple florets growing on bare stems up to 120 cm (4 ft) tall.

This species is best used in small groups among medium-height perennials. It is essential to provide cover in winter. It is planted at a depth of 10 cm (4 in.) and at distances of 25–30 cm (10–12 in.).

Allium karataviense

Allium moly

ALLIUM KARATAVIENSE

This allium, which originates in Turkestan, is a truly remarkable species. Its inflorescence, a globular, many-flowered umbel, resembles the species illustrated on the previous page, but in this case the 'globe' is somewhat smaller and the stem is very short — at most 20–30 cm (8–12 in.). The bulb often produces only two shiny, grey-green and red-edged leaves. Such decorative leaves are very rare among alliums. Nearly all other species are downright ugly when not in flower. The flowers appear in May. This allium shows best in a rock-garden in association with, for instance, Euphorbia polythroma (greenish-yellow).

We plant in October at a depth of $\pm$ 6–7 cm (2–2$\frac{1}{2}$ in.).

ALLIUM MOLY

It is always difficult to determine which species of a particular genus is cultivated and used most often. In the case of allium this is almost certainly this yellow-flowering form, partly, of course, because the striking little white bulbs are cheap to buy. The fact that they may be left *in situ* for many years also plays a part.

The star-shaped yellow flowers, placed in umbels, appear in June and July. The height of the plant is about 25 cm (10 in.). This allium can be used for cutting as well as in the border.

The dry chalk hills and alpine meadows of South-western Europe are the plant's natural habitat.

Allium neapolitanum

Allium oreophilum

ALLIUM NEAPOLITANUM (White Garlic)

The pure white, slender umbels of Allium neapolitanum appear in May or June; they have a pleasant scent. The species, which reaches a height of about 30 cm (12 in.) is a native of the Mediterranean area.

Did you know that a beautiful allium species grows wild in this country? This species, A. ursinum, or Ransoms, also has white flowers and still occurs in woods. Well-stocked firms will be able to supply the bulbs. Allium ursinum is suitable for naturalisation. Since we are talking about white-flowered allium species, we should not neglect to mention A. triquetrum. This rare species, which has triangular stems, grows to a height of around 50 cm (20 in.)

ALLIUM OREOPHILUM

All the allium species illustrated or mentioned here prefer moisture-retaining soil and nearly all like a sunny situation. A. oreophilum, often called A. ostrowskianum, is no exception.

The plant originates in Eastern Turkestan, a country which has been of great importance to lovers of bulbs, for a remarkably large number of species grow wild there.

The carmine umbels appearing in June grow on stems of about 20 cm (8 in.).

As you see, there is a wide range of allium species. Remember there are many more, for instance the blue A. caeruleum and the tall, rose-purple A. sphaerocephalum.

Anemone blanda

Anemone coronaria 'de Caen'

ANEMONE BLANDA

After the snowdrops and the winter aconites, the anemones of the blanda species (the word means charming or beautiful) appear to remind us that spring is round the corner. They do so in a most prolific manner. It seems as if the small white, pink and blue, daisy-shaped flowers have been scattered over the ground with a liberal hand. This feast to the eyes takes place in March or April. As the tubers, native of the Caucasus and Asia Minor, are completely hardy, they may be left undisturbed in their corner of the garden for many years. We plant the unusually shaped tubers in October–November at a depth of 7 cm (3 in.). The plants, which tolerate a certain amount of shade, grow to only 10–20 cm (4–8 in.).

ANEMONE CORONARIA

No doubt you are familiar with the well-known anemone 'de Caen' with its blue, red, violet and white flowers. In winter and spring these large, well-shaped flowers, which frequently have black stamens, are often sold in flower shops.

Apart from the single-flowered forms, there are double and semi-double varieties as well. The latter are known as 'St. Brigid' anemones.

These anemones, whose native habitat is the Mediterranean area, are also very suitable as garden plants; they flower in June–July. They grow to ± 30 cm (12 in.) and like fertile, moisture-retaining soil. Plant in March at a depth of 5–8 cm (2–3 in.). Once the plants have died down it is advisable to lift the strangely shaped tubers. It is possible to store them, but flowering declines. They will flower in September also, if planted in June, or in late winter–spring, if planted in autumn.

Anemone nemorosa

Anemone pavonina 'St. Bavo'

ANEMONE NEMOROSA (Wood anemone)

Not many bulbous and tuberous plants in this book form part of our indigenous flora, but the wood anemone is one which does.

This woodland plant, which is found everywhere above the equator, has a creeping rootstock and is suitable for naturalisation in the garden. In March—April it produces white flowers, pink or mauve on the outside. From the stem grow three sharply-indented leaves. The hand-shaped compound leaf develops only during or just after flowering. It is most important to plant the rhizomes immediately they are received, for they dry out very quickly.

Plant in autumn to a depth of $\pm$ 5–7 cm (2–3 in.) in a moist soil.

ANEMONE PAVONINA

'Multipetala' and 'St. Bavo' are the best known strains of this species; there are considerable differences between the two. The former has flowers consisting of a large number of small orange-red petals on stems about 25 cm (10 in.) in height; they appear in May. The 'St. Bavo' anemone, introduced by Messrs. Tubergen of Haarlem, has fewer but wider petals in various colours.

Light covering in winter is advisable for both cultivars. We plant them in a sunny position in well-drained soil at a distance of 10 cm (4 in.) and a depth of 8 cm (3 in.). The second half of October or early November is often given as the best time for planting. Lift at the end of July and keep dry until they are replanted.

Begonia boliviensis 'Cascade'

Begonia grandiflora

BEGONIA BOLIVIENSIS

Botanically the three tuberous begonias illustrated and described here belong to the species B. tuberhybrida. These hybrids have been created by crossing various South American species. The pointed-flowered boliviensis type clearly shows the characteristics of the original native of Bolivia. It is pendulous in habit and is often sold for use in baskets. The flowers are small to medium in size, single or double, and have typically pointed petals. Unfortunately we rarely see this begonia in this country; a great pity, for it is certainly no less beautiful than the generally used large- and small-flowered forms. It flourishes in a window-box out of direct sunlight.

BEGONIA GRANDIFLORA (Large- flowered tuberous begonia)

Numerous forms may be distinguished, but the ordinary double-flowered form is seen most often. Although red begonias are perhaps the most popular, they occur also in pink, white, yellow and orange.

Tuberous begonias are cultivated on a large scale in the area round Ghent, in Belgium. In summer the fields of flowering plants attract many visitors.

Tuberous begonias are very suitable for planting in beds, but can also be used in borders. A half-shady position and moisture-retaining soil rich in humus are most suitable. Large-flowered begonias should be planted at distances of 25 cm (10 in.). They grow to a height of about 25 cm (10 in.) and flower from June until the first night-frosts, particularly if dead flowers are regularly removed.

Begonia multiflora

Bletilla striata

BEGONIA MULTIFLORA (Small-flowered tuberous begonia)

All tuberous begonias are very sensitive to frost — after all, they originated in South America. It is therefore wrong to plant them out of doors too early in the year.

There are two methods of planting. Some gardeners place the tubers in trays containing moist peat fibre in March or early April, putting the trays in a greenhouse or frame. From June 1st onwards the tubers, which by then have developed shoots, are planted out of doors. Another method is to plant the tubers 'blind' in early May. These tubers, which have not previously been started into growth, are covered with only $\frac{1}{2}$ cm (a sprinkling) of soil. One of the finest small-flowered begonias is 'Flamboyant' (scarlet). It grows to a height of 20 cm (8 in.) and flowers profusely. Towards November the tubers are lifted, dried and stored in a dry, fairly cool but frost-free place until the following year. Large tubers may be cut up, provided each piece has some eyes.

BLETILLA STRIATA

Of the orchid family, which numbers at least 18,000 species, only a few are suitable for growing in the garden. Several species are native to this country, but they are not supplied for sale. Please do not dig them up in the wild; your chances of success in growing them afterwards are very slight and we should conserve them by all means at our disposal. The best known and most easily cultivated species is Bletilla striata (sometimes called Bletia hyacinthina). It originates in Eastern Asia. This orchid is reasonably tolerant of cold, but give it some protection during the winter. The plant, which grows to 30—50 cm (12—20 in.), flowers in June—July. Partial shade is desirable. Plant the tubers in spring at a depth of 4—5 cm ($1\frac{3}{4}$—2 in.).

Camassia cusickii

Canna hybrid

CAMASSIA (Quamash)

Species belonging to this genus occur in the Western part of North America. They are excellent border plants, but are also suitable for naturalisation, especially in partial shade. The globular or pear-shaped bulbs should be planted in October at a depth of 8 cm (3 in.).

Camassia quamash (syn. C. esculenta) has violet coloured flowers growing on stems of 30–50 cm (12–20 in.). It is the latest flowering species, blooming in June–July.

Camassia cusickii, on the other hand, flowers as early as April–May. Its star-shaped flowers are pale blue. Its height is ± 75 cm (2½ ft).

Camassia leichtlinii, finally, flowers in May. The cream-coloured flowers are placed in dense racemes. The stems may grow to as much as 100 cm (3½ ft).

CANNA HYBRIDA (Indian shot)

Indian shot (it used to be called Canna indica) is very demanding as regards soil and position. Rich, moisture-retaining soil and a sheltered, sunny situation are essential. The rhizomes are potted in early April in rich compost and started into growth in a greenhouse at a temperature of ± 20° C (68° F). After the plants have been hardened off they can be placed in a border in early June. Rhizomes which have not previously been started into growth may be planted out of doors in late May. It is essential to place them at least 50 cm (20 in.) apart. In autumn the plants are lifted and stored, together with the adhering soil, in an airy place which must not be too cool. Canna has green or bronze foliage and flowers in the colours yellow, pink, orange and red. Apart from the tall varieties, up to 150 cm (5 ft), there are also dwarf forms.

Chionodoxa luciliae

Chionodoxa sardensis

CHIONODOXA LUCILIAE (Glory of the snow)

Glory of the snow is a completely hardy, profusely flowering bulbous plant, a native of Asia Minor. The common name indicates the flowering period. This falls in March and although we prefer to be free of snow in that month, the name is nevertheless a good choice.

The Chionodoxa luciliae species illustrated above has numerous flowers to each stem. Height is about 15 cm (6 in.). There are also white and purplish-red forms. The cultivar 'Pink Giant' is much in demand because of its large, bright pink flowers and vigorous growth.

Although the flowers of another species, C. gigantea, are larger, they are fewer in number. Its colour is pale violet-blue, sometimes with, sometimes without a small white eye.

CHIONODOXA SARDENSIS

The bulbs of the various species of Glory of the snow, which are relatively small and cheap, are planted at the end of September or the beginning of October at a depth of 5 cm (2 in.).

They can be left undisturbed for many years and in favourable conditions spread freely. Not only do they develop new bulbs, but their seed also grows into new plants.

Chionodoxa sardensis is rather different from the other species illustrated and described. We should also mention C. tmolusii. The flowers of this species are white with violet tips to the petals.

Some species of Glory of the snow are suitable for growing indoors at low temperatures.

Colchicum autumnale

Colchicum bulbocodium

COLCHICUM AUTUMNALE (Meadow saffron or Naked boys)

Many amateur gardeners mistake the colchicum for a crocus. One important difference is that the meadow saffron has six, and the crocus only three stamens. This means that they in fact belong to two different families (Liliaceae and Iridaceae respectively). The flowers come in September, but the leaves are not produced until spring. It is very important not to cut the foliage off, but to let it die down naturally in July.

Colchicum should be planted in July at a depth of 10 cm (4 in.). Give them plenty of room, for they develop a fair amount of foliage (15–20 cm (6–8 in.) apart).

Meadow saffrons are preferably planted among trees and shrubs and allowed to naturalise. In September they will flower indoors near a window without soil or water. After flowering they may still be planted in the garden.

COLCHICUM BULBOCODIUM

This species is better known under the name Bulbocodium vernum. Vernum means 'flowering in spring', whereas Colchicum makes us think of the well-known meadow saffron which flowers in September and October. However, this is not the only spring-flowering form.

The pale violet flowers emerge from the cold soil as early as February or March, before the foliage is far developed.

We plant in early October at a depth of 7–8 cm (3–3½ in.). The tubers may be left undisturbed in the ground for several years.

This tuberous plant, which grows wild in the Pyrenees and elsewhere, is completely hardy. You are strongly advised to give it a try.

Convallaria majalis

Corbularia (Narcissus) bulbocodium

CONVALLARIA MAJALIS (Lily of the valley)

Lilies of the valley are very useful for planting in the garden as well as for marketing as cut flowers. They are sold all the year round, as their cultivation can be advanced as well as retarded.

This woodland plant, which will flourish even in fairly deep shade, is much in demand, especially for underplanting. In favourable conditions (soil rich in humus and moderately (moist) the plants will spread vigorously.

The name indicates its flowering period: majalis means May-flowering. The wide, bell-shaped florets have a delicious scent. There may be as many as 12 to the stalk, which may grow to 20 cm (8 in.). The rhizomes, with their points (buds) showing, are planted in autumn or early spring. The soil over the points should not exceed 1 cm ($\frac{1}{2}$ in.).

CORBULARIA (NARCISSUS) BULBOCODIUM (Hoop-petticoat daffodil)

This small bulbous plant is warmly recommented for people who like something unusual. Its natural habitat is in the marshy meadows of the Mediterranean area.

As the flowers, which appear in April, are very small, it is essential to plant them where they will catch the eye. They show up best against a rock, a wall or in front of a not too rampant evergreen plant.

Plant in autumn in groups of at least 15, at a depth of only 3 cm (1 in.). In winter light protection is advisable for this plant, which grows to 12 cm (5 in.). They are also very attractive if naturalised in grass.

Corydalis solida

Crinum x powellii

CORYDALIS SOLIDA (Fumitory)

As well as this species, other forms of the genus Corydalis are often seen in gardens, namely C. lutea (yellow fumitory) and C. cava.

Fumitory is a small tuberous woodland plant occurring from Western Europe as far east as Northern Asia. It grows wild or in a naturalised state in this country as well, albeit rarely. In the garden the spurred purple flowers come up in large quantities in the period March—April. As it is a woodland plant the tubers may be planted under not too dense trees and shrubs; this is done in October at a depth of 6—7 cm (2—2½ in.). In other words, this is another plant suitable for naturalisation.

The flowers of corydalis are much frequented by wild bees such as the Sachem bee (Anthophora).

CRINUM X POWELLII

Crinum bulbs are large and unusually bottle-shaped with a long neck. The hybrid C. powellii is the result of crossing C. bulbispermum and C. moorei, both natives of Africa.

Most representatives of this genus must be cultivated in a cold or heated glasshouse. C. x powellii, however, may be grown out of doors as well, provided it is given a sheltered and warm position and rich soil.

The large, beautifully shaped and fragrant flowers appear in late summer.

The bulbs are planted in spring in such a way that the neck projects from the soil. They must be well protected in winter. There is also a white cultivar.

Crocosmia crocosmiiflora

*Crocus chrysanthus 'Blue Pearl' (left),
'Cream Beauty' (right)*

CROCOSMIA CROCOSMIIFLORA

This member of the iris family, better known as montbretia, originates in South Africa. There are large-flowered as well as small-flowered cultivars in the colours yellow, orange, red and numerous shades in between. The flowers appear in August and September; the stems are 60–90 cm (2–3 ft) tall.

Although montbretia is most valuable for cutting, it is also a brilliant border plant.

Planting of the corms takes place in April at a depth of $\pm$ 8 cm (3 in.).

Moisture-retaining, rich soil and a sunny situation are essential. Provided they are well protected in winter, they may be left undisturbed for many years.

CROCUS CHRYSANTHUS

Among the species crocuses this one is undoubtedly the most often cultivated. The original form, nowadays largely neglected, is yellow (*vide* the specific name chrysanthus, meaning 'with golden yellow flowers'). Asia Minor and the Balkans are the native habitats of these flowers.

Crocus chrysanthus differs from most other species in the round shape of the flowers.

There are about 40 cultivars of this species. Some excellent ones are: 'Snowbunting' (white), 'Cream Beauty' (cream), 'E. P. Bowles' (yellow), and 'Blue Pearl' (pale violet-blue, white inside). The small corms are planted in October at a depth of 5–6 cm (about 2 in.). Do try this species; success is assured.

Crocus etruscus 'Zwanenburg'

Crocus flavus 'Luteus'

CROCUS ETRUSCUS

The main advantage of species crocuses over the so-called hybrid crocuses is the fact that they flower earlier and often more profusely. Although the flowers are rather small, their number more than compensates for this. Moreover, the foliage has hardly begun to develop at the time of flowering. It is therefore advisable to plant large quantities in order to achieve a good effect.

Crocus etruscus is a native of Central Italy and is nowadays rarely cultivated. The cultivar of this called 'Zwanenburg', bred by Messrs. Tubergen, has brilliant violet-blue flowers.

A close relation is Crocus sieberi, which comes from Greece. The cultivar 'Violet Queen' has purple flowers with a bronze-coloured base to each petal.

CROCUS FLAVUS (Dutch yellow crocus)

There is no doubt that the large yellow crocuses are the most beloved of all. This is probably mainly due to their colour, for yellow is a colour we all like to see in spring as being a harbinger of the coming summer. Just think how many yellow-flowering plants brighten the gardens early in the year.

Unfortunately sparrows are of the same mind, for they adore these crocuses, although they may go for other colours (for lack of something better?). To prevent this destruction black cotton can be stretched across the plants.

The corms of the yellow crocus differ somewhat from those of other colours. Treatment is the same.

Crocus speciosus

Crocus tomasinianus

CROCUS SPECIOSUS (Autumn crocus)

For lovers of the unusual there are several species of autumn-flowering crocus. Nevertheless they are rarely used, probably because planting takes place in July and August – who thinks of planting bulbs in the holiday period? Nevertheless you should give them a try – they are well worth it. It is true that their colours are not very striking, but the profusion and the time of their flowering (September–October) makes up for this.

There are many species. C. speciosus, illustrated above, occurs, among other places, in eastern Europe; there are many cultivars of this species available. C. kotschyanus (syn. C. zonatus), lilac-pink in colour, is also worth mentioning.

CROCUS TOMASINIANUS

All the so-called species spring-flowering crocuses mentioned here must be planted in September–October at a depth of 6–7 cm (about 3 in.) and at distances of between 8 and 12 cm (3 and 5 in.), depending on the size of the corms. Like all other crocuses they may be left undisturbed in the ground for many years.

Of the C. tomasinianus, which is a native of the Balkans, there is also a cultivar called 'Whitewell Purple' on the market, which is considerably darker in colour than the original species. Both are characterised by their truly superabundant flowering. They can hardly be bettered for naturalising.

Although crocuses are hardy, a light covering of leaves in severe frost may protect damage to the young shoots.

Crocus 'Remembrance'

Crocus 'Pickwick'

CROCUS VERNUS HYBRIDS

The crocuses illustrated on this page are hybrid or Dutch garden crocuses. C. vernus, which grows wild in the Pyrenees, the Alps, the Jura and elsewhere, has played an important part in the development of these hybrids.

Crocuses can be used in all kinds of ways. We see them in borders and rock gardens, but also in lawns, and naturalised under trees. Occasionally they are even used in window-boxes and for bedding. The marketable sizes vary between 7 and 11, the figures indicating the circumference of the corm in centimetres (inches). It is advisable to plant the larger sizes. Several flowers will develop from each pip (young shoot) of the corm.

Hybrid crocuses are generally planted in the period October–November at a depth of 6–8 cm ($2\frac{1}{2}$–$3\frac{1}{2}$ in.). To achieve a dense effect, about 100 to 125 corms should be planted per square metre (square yard). Be careful if using fresh manure, of which they are very intolerant. After the flowering period (March–April) it is interesting to study the seed formation. During flowering the ovary is underground, but when seed formation begins ($1\frac{1}{2}$–2 months after flowering) the ovary appears above ground to enable the seeds to ripen.

Among the most valuable blue kinds are: 'Remembrance' (blue, early, large-flowered), 'Queen of the Blues' (soft blue), 'Early Perfection' (early, blue-mauve), 'Enchantress' (pale mauve with a silver sheen) and 'Purpureus Grandiflorus' (purple, medium-sized, early). 'Jeanne d'Arc' (large-flowered, early and profuse) and 'Peter Pan' (a little later and somewhat smaller) are good white crocuses. Among the so-called striped crocuses 'Pickwick' and 'Striped Beauty' should be mentioned.

Cyclamen coum

Cyclamen europaeum

CYCLAMEN COUM

The Cyclamen persicum, at least in its large-flowering forms, is very well known as a pot plant. It is marketed in enormous quantities, especially during the winter period. It is less well known that there are also some which are suitable for planting in the garden.

These cyclamen species are divided into two large groups, namely spring-flowering and autumn-flowering forms.

Cyclamen coum, of which the 'Roseum' form is illustrated, is a native of Asia Minor. The pink or red flowers appear as early as February—March.

The species, of which many cultivars are grown, is usually cultivated in a cold frame, since the weather is often fatal to the beautiful flowers. Autumn is the time of planting.

CYCLAMEN EUROPAEUM

This species is easy to grow and is more readily obtainable than the previous one. The plants occur wild in sub-alpine mountains. They flower profusely, especially after the plants have been left undisturbed for some years; the flowering period is around September.

Rich, moisture-retaining soil, preferably containing some humus, and partial shade, provide ideal growing conditions.

A sheltered position and a light mulch of straw or similar material in winter increase the chances of good results. The corms are usually planted in spring at a depth of only 1—2 cm ($\frac{1}{2}$ in.).

No flowers can be expected in the first year.

Dahlia — anemone-flowered mixed

Dahlia — cactus-type 'Border Princess'

DAHLIA HYBRIDS

The co-called Anemone-flowered dahlia differs from the Mignon type by its fairly long tubular florets. It is not very often grown, and this is a pity, for its unusual inflorescence distinguishes it from other species and makes it more striking.

Planting distances vary considerably among the various dahlia groups. Tall-growing cultivars need distances of over 50—60 cm (20—24 in.), whereas 20 cm (8 in.) is sufficient for the small Topmix dahlia.

Among Anemone-flowered dahlias some valuable cultivars are: 'Bridesmaid' (white/cream), 'Honey' (bronze/yellow), 'Guinea' (yellow), 'Siemen Doorenbosch' (pink/white) and 'Raspberry Flan' (cerise/yellow).

DAHLIA HYBRIDS — CACTUS-FLOWERING

The dahlia originates in Mexico. The plant was described in a Spanish book as early as the beginning of the seventeenth century. Nevertheless it was not until the early nineteenth century that the dahlia made its triumphal march throughout Europe. In the course of the years it has conquered practically every garden.

The petals of the Cactus-flowering dahlia are rolled up into tubes — we sometimes say it has a spider-shape. The importance of this group as a whole is slightly on the decrease. Apart from the 'Border Princess' illustrated, the following cultivars can be recommended: 'Curtain Raiser' (peach-coloured), 'Priscilla' (reddish-orange), 'Klankstad Kerkrade' (creamy yellow), 'Top Choice' (red and yellow) and 'Gold Crown' (golden bronze).

Dahlia – decorative-type 'Arabian Night'

Dahlia – Collarette-type – mixed

DAHLIA HYBRIDS – DECORATIVE

The Decorative dahlia is particularly popular for cutting, but it is also in its element in the border. Most cultivars in this group have large flowers and reach considerable heights, to 150 cm (5 ft). However, there are also some smaller-flowered and lower-growing forms: these are sometimes called Miniature Decorative dahlias. They may also be used for bedding. All Decorative dahlias are double-flowered and have wide, flattish petals. Good cultivars are 'Arabian Night' (black/red), 'Gerrie Hoek' (pink), 'Glorie van Heemstede' (yellow), 'Lavender Perfection' (lilac), 'Red and White' (red, white-tipped), 'Snow Country' (white), 'Rosella' (pink), 'Holland Festival' (orange, white-tipped), 'Giraffe' (corn yellow, brown stripes), 'Chinese Lantern' (clear orange-red) and 'Rocquencourt' (orange-black foliage, low-growing, orange flowers with an amber glow).

DAHLIA HYBRIDS – COLLARETTE

The Collarette dahlia has much in common with the Mignon type. The outer row of tubular florets, about half the size of the petals, form a 'collar'. As this collar is often of a different colour, it stands out all the more. This dahlia grows to 75–100 cm (30–40 in.); planting distance is around 40 cm (16 in.).

Some bestsellers among the Collarettes are: 'La Cierva' (purple with white), 'Grand Duc' (red, white and yellow) and 'Kaiser Walzer' (orange-red with yellow).

Dahlia cuttings should be planted late in the second half of May. Tubers which have been stored through the winter may be planted earlier, namely towards the end of April. Make sure they have a sunny position, for they cannot live without sun.

Dahlia – mignon-type 'Irene v.d. Zwet'   *Dahlia – pompon-type 'Kochelsee'*

DAHLIA HYBRIDS – MIGNON or single-flowered

The Mignon dahlia is almost certainly the form best loved by gardeners. Not surprising, for the striking single flowers, the beautiful colours and the prolonged flowering period are all valuable characteristics. They have recently been reclassified, and are now known as single-flowered.

They are often used for bedding and may also be planted in narrow borders. A sunny situation and rich soil are essential to achieve best results with all the groups of dahlias discussed here. Most cultivars grow to 40–50 cm (16–20 in.). Very good strains are: 'G. F. Hemerik' (orange), 'Irene van der Zwet' (soft yellow), 'Nelly Geerlings' (red), 'Sneezy' (white), and 'Murillo' (mauve-pink with a dark ring).

DAHLIA HYBRIDS – POMPON

The Pompon dahlia has a practically circular inflorescence and the separate petals are clearly funnel-shaped. The plants may easily reach a height of 100 cm (40 in.) or more. For this reason they are often planted at the back of a border; they also possess good qualities for cutting. The taller forms usually require staking; this should be done in good time. The plant will to some extent adapt itself to the stake, which will produce a more natural effect.

Good cultivars among Pompons are: 'Kochelsee' (red), 'Magnificat' (orange/red), 'Pride of Berlin' (mauve-pink), 'Mark Lockwood' (light mauve), 'Deepest Yellow' (yellow) and 'Wee Joy' (soft orange).

Dahlia — semi-cactus-type 'Purity'

Dahlia — topmix-type — mixed

DAHLIA HYBRIDS – SEMI-CACTUS

The Semi-cactus dahlia may be regarded as an intermediate form between the Cactus-flowered and the Decorative dahlias. For cutting purposes the dahlias of this group can hardly be bettered. They should be cut dry, when the flowers are fully out; this should preferably be done early in the morning or late in the evening.

There are a great many cultivars. Every year numerous new forms appear on the market. In mentioning names I have sought the advice of Mr. Maarse of Aalsmeer, one of the greatest specialists in this field. Only those cultivars will be referred to which have already proven their worth: 'Popular Guest' (pink), 'Rotterdam' (dark red), 'Beauty of Aalsmeer' (salmon pink), 'Bacchus' (red), 'Gina Lombaert' (salmon pink with a yellow heart), 'Park Princess' (pink, miniature), and 'Purity' (white).

DAHLIA HYBRIDS – TOPMIX

Dwarf dahlias form a relatively new group. They grow to only 20–30 cm (8–12 in.) and have small flowers in a variety of colours. The stems are particularly firm. Topmix dahlias may be used in window-boxes, beds and borders. The flowering period is prolonged, namely from June till October. Interest in these dahlias has been increasing in recent years.

'Bonne Esperance' (pink), 'Reddy' (red), 'Bambino' (white) and 'Chessy' (yellow) have fully proven their worth in the garden; collections of mixed colours are also available.

As is the case with all dahlias, the tubers may be lifted in October and when dry can successfully be stored in dry peat in a dry, frost-free place.

Eranthis cilicica

Eremurus x shelford

ERANTHIS CILICICA (Winter aconite)

The yellow flowers of the winter aconite can be enjoyed before any of the other bulbous or tuberous plants appear, with the exception of the snowdrop. In mild winters this can be as early as February. By planting the tubers together with other subjects suitable for under-planting, such as snowdrops, species crocuses, Lenten roses and Anemone blanda, we can achieve a colourful variety of flowers very early in the year.

We plant them, preferably at the end of September—early October, at a depth of $\pm$ 5 cm (2 in.). In the first year flowering may be somewhat disappointing, but subsequent years will more than make up for this. Apart from the Eranthis cilicica illustrated above, there is a species with the suitable specific name hyemalis, meaning 'winter-flowering'.

EREMURUS X SHELFORD (Foxtail lily)

There are few tubers so strangely shaped as those of the eremurus. I think they look rather like spiders or daddy-long-legs. In fact they consist of a very short stem with a large bud and a number of horizontally placed fleshy roots.

The tubers should be planted as soon as they reach you in August or September, at a depth of 10 cm (4 in.). Make sure the roots are not damaged and are spread out properly, preferably on a bed of coarse sand. Planting distance varies between 30 and 60 cm (12 and 24 in.), depending on the species. Eremurus is excellent for cutting as well as for planting in the border. A spot in the sun and well-drained soil are essential for good development. Flowering takes place mainly in May—June. There are several species, differing in height, 50—200 cm ($1\frac{1}{2}$—8 ft) and in colour (white, pink, yellow, orange, brown).

54

Erythronium dens-canis

Erythronium revolutum 'White Beauty'

ERYTHRONIUM DENS-CANIS (Dog's-tooth violet)

Apart from its fine, drooping pink flowers, the dog's-tooth violet has beautifully marked foliage. The plants are decorative even when not in flower, something which can be said of few other bulbous and tuberous plants.

The common name 'dog's tooth' is a literal translation of the botanical name. The plant owes this appellation to the very strangely shaped little bulbs which do, in fact, resemble teeth.

This species occurs wild in the mountain forests and meadows of Central and Southern Europe. They like moisture-retaining soil and partial shade. The plant, which grows to 15 cm (6 in.), flowers in March–April.

ERYTHRONIUM REVOLUTUM

Unlike the previous species, this erythronium is a native of California. It has considerably larger flowers, a later flowering time and grows somewhat taller. In the rock-garden, where it is often used, it is a much more striking plant.

It is extremely important to plant the bulbs of all this genus immediately you receive them (September–October), for they dry out very rapidly.

In the first year flowering is often disappointing, or even altogether absent. Since they can be left in the ground, and flowering consequently becomes increasingly profuse, this does not present too great a disadvantage.

'White Beauty' is a magnificent, pure white cultivar. 'Pagoda' is yellow in colour. It belongs to the species E. tuolumnense.

Eucomis bicolor

Freesia hybrids — mixed

EUCOMIS BICOLOR

If you want to give this very unusual plant a place in your garden, you will have to browse through the catalogues. You will not find it in all of them; only a very well stocked grower will be able to supply it.

You should plant the bulbs in April at a depth of about 8–10 cm (3–4 in.). The large leaves appear first, to be followed towards the end of summer by a stem with red-edged, greenish flowers. The tuft of leaves at the top of the flower-spike gives an amusing effect. The plant, which is a native of South Africa, reaches a height of 50 cm (20 in.). In winter the bulbs must be stored in a frost-free place. Eucomis looks well in the perennial border, especially in association with yellow-flowering plants (e.g. rudbeckia and helenium).

FREESIA HYBRIDS

Strange as it may appear, the freesia likes a cool situation. What is more, if, in the period after planting, the temperature of the soil is too high, flowering will be postponed. Freesia is one of the most important cut flowers. Many are grown every year for the trade in cool greenhouses, especially in the Lea Valley and the South of England.

Although outdoor cultivation does not produce nearly such splendid flowers, they are nevertheless useful for planting on a small scale in the garden, if only for their delicious scent.

They should be planted at a depth of $\pm$ 5 cm (2 in.) as soon as possible after you have received them, in April or early May.

The flowering period is July—August. They are usually sold as a mixture. The corms cannot be used a second year, as they are pre-treated to flower in summer instead of winter.

Fritillaria imperialis 'Lutea' *Fritillaria meleagris*

FRITILLARIA IMPERIALIS (Crown Imperial)

A very apt name for this majestic plant from the Himalayas.

It is advisable to plant the large, expensive bulbs as soon as you receive them, for they have a very unpleasant smell.

The flowers, orange, orange-red or yellow, appear in April–May. The plants may easily grow to 100 cm (3½ ft).

It is necessary to give them sufficient space: a distance of 20–30 cm (8–12 in.) is not too much. Depth of planting should be at least 10–12 cm (4–5 in.).

FRITILLARIA MELEAGRIS (Snake's-head fritillary, Guinea-hen flower)

The snake's-head fritillary still occurs wild, although very rarely, in damp riverside spots.

The unusually marked, purple flowers appear in April–May on stems of about 20–25 cm (8–10 in.). Bulbs are planted in October at a depth of 5–6 cm (about 2 in.) and will give us pleasure for many years. They feel most at home in not-too-dry soil and in partial shade. Never use fresh manure when planting.

The snake's-head fritillary is particularly suitable for livening up certain ground-covering plants. I once saw them growing with great effect among the rather sombre green Pachysandra terminalis.

Galanthus nivalis

Galtonia candicans

GALANTHUS NIVALIS (Snowdrop)

There cannot be many people who do not know the snowdrop. Hardly surprising, since few herbaceous plants flower so early in the year.

The drooping little white flowers appear as early as February; the stems are about 15 cm (6 in.) tall. The snowdrop grows wild in the meadows and forests of Europe, the Caucasus and Asia Minor, and has been cultivated since 1500.

Snowdrops should be planted in large clumps, especially under shrubs and trees, and in lawns. In the latter case some shade is desirable. Galanthus elwesii is a species with broader leaves and somewhat larger flowers. The best times to plant are just after they have flowered, or as early as possible in autumn.

GALTONIA CANDICANS (Summer-flowering hyacinth)

Galtonia really does resemble the hyacinth somewhat. The species originates in Natal, South Africa.

It is a fairly tall plant, over 100 cm (3½ ft). The stems bear numerous drooping flowers, sweet-scented like those of the hyacinth. A sunny position is essential.

The large bulbs should be planted in April in a sunny place, and well-drained soil, at a depth of 13 cm (5 in.). The best way to use the plant is in the perennial border. Its flowering period (August—September) means that it will provide a good display in combination with Michaelmas daisies, helenium, phlox, rudbeckia and salvia. The bulbs should be disturbed as little as possible after planting, lifting only when they show signs of deterioration.

58

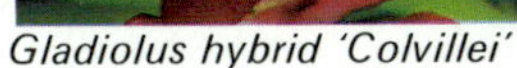

Gladiolus hybrid 'Colvillei'

Gladiolus 'Sans Souci'

GLADIOLUS HYBRIDS – 'COLVILLEI'

Unfortunately 'Colvillei' gladioli are not always easily obtainable. A pity, for this plant, a result of crossing many species, is certainly worth growing.

It belongs to the group of small-flowered gladiolus hybrids. It should be planted as late in the year as possible, preferably in the first week of December, in order to reduce to a minimum the risk that they will come up too soon and be damaged by frost.

Depth of planting is ± 8 cm (3 in.) and they should be well protected in winter.

The white, pink or red flowers appear in June; the stems grow to 60–70 cm (24–28 in.). They are popular for cutting.

GLADIOLUS HYBRIDS – 'GANDAVENSIS'

To avoid disease do not plant gladioli in the same spot in consecutive years.

Pick a somewhat sheltered sunny situation and make sure the soil contains sufficient nourishment. Plant in April at a depth of 6–8 cm (2½–3½ in.) and about 10 cm (4 in.) apart. When flowering (July–August), they may reach a height of as much as 100–150 cm (3½–5 ft).

You might reserve a corner for them where they can be grown for cutting. The beautifully shaped flowers of these large-flowered hybrids are a feast for the eye, especially if arranged in a mixture of colours, for instance in a large copper jug. Some especially good ones to give a variety of colour are 'Flower Song' (yellow), 'Mabel Violet', 'Mansoer' (velvety black/red), 'New Europe' (red), 'Peter Pears' (tangerine), 'Snow Princess', 'Toulouse-Lautrec' (apricot, orange and yellow).

It is not always easy to store the corms which must be kept perfectly dry.

Gladiolus nanus

Hyacinthus 'Carnegie'

GLADIOLUS NANUS

This species is available in various colours, such as light and dark red, pale and dark pink, and white.

It grows only to about 40 cm (16 in.) and flowers in June—July. There are fewer flowers per stem than is the case with other species, but the plant is more graceful. Time and depth of planting, etc., are the same as in the case of the Colvillei gladioli mentioned previously.

For fanatical searchers for the unusual I should like to mention G. byzantinus. This is a hardy species originating in the Mediterranean area. The reddish-purple flowers come out from June onwards. Height around 60 cm (2 ft).

HYACINTHUS HYBRID – WHITE

The native habitat of the fragrant hyacinth (Hyacinthus orientalis) is in the neighbourhood of Baghdad and Aleppo. The first bulbs were brought to Western Europe as early as the middle of the sixteenth century.

The wild species has only 6—12 florets to each spike. The colour of this species, which is not cultivated, is violet-blue.

A white form developed many centuries ago, and to this day white hyacinths are very popular. Many specialists consider 'Carnegie', illustrated above, to be the best for garden purposes. We should also mention 'L'Innocence', which comes up earlier.

60

Hyacinthus 'City of Haarlem'

Hyacinthus 'Jan Bos'

HYACINTHUS HYBRID – YELLOW

Yellow-flowering hyacinths are comparatively rare. They are not really yellow, although the colour of 'Yellow Hammer' is better than that of 'City of Haarlem' illustrated above. If you like something unusual I would recommend the former, but they are not often grown nowadays.

Nearly all hyacinths do best in coarse-grained, chalky soil, poor in humus. In areas where it is not like this, it can be improved by adding well-rotted organic matter, such as garden compost or leafmould, some weeks before planting.

Hyacinths demand a sunny situation. If you want to keep bulbs for planting the following year, it is advisable to cut off the flower-spikes immediately after flowering. Store the bulbs in a fairly warm place (20–25° C (68–78° F). Don't expect too much of these second-year bulbs, however.

HYACINTHUS HYBRID – RED

Although 'Jan Bos' is the red hyacinth most often cultivated, it is not the most suitable for the garden. Because in the greenhouse it can be made to flower early (growers call this 'forcing'), 'Jan Bos' is much in demand in the trade. One great disadvantage is that the top of the inflorescence consists of green florets. 'Jan Bos' also does not always breed true to colour.

'Tubergen's Scarlet', carmine to scarlet, with fairly small flowers, and 'Amsterdam', dark salmon-red and early-flowering, are to be preferred.

For planting in the garden you should choose the smaller-sized bulbs. They are less expensive and the spikes will not topple so easily.

Hyacinthus 'Lord Balfour'

Hyacinthus 'Ostara'

HYACINTHUS HYBRID – PURPLE

The number of purple hyacinths is not large. Nevertheless some people prefer this colour, perhaps because it looks well in combination with other colours, for instance yellow. 'Amethyst' is the purple cultivar grown on the largest scale. Talking of unusual hyacinth colours, I should like to draw your attention to another rare one, namely 'Oranje Boven', which has an unusual salmon-orange colour.

As hyacinths are somewhat ungraceful for planting in the border, I would advise you to buy small size bulbs for this purpose, 14–15 and 15–16 cm (5–5½ and 6–6½ in.). These will produce small spikes with few florets, which will not look out of place.

HYACINTHUS HYBRID – BLUE

Blue hyacinths form a very important group. There are numerous useful cultivars, both for forcing and for the garden.

For the sake of convenience we divide this group into three, namely dark blue, medium blue and pale blue.

Some of the best in the first category are 'Marie' and 'Blue Jacket'. Among the medium-blue varieties we should mention 'Delft Blue' and 'Ostara'. 'Fürst Bismarck' also belongs to this group, but sometimes suffers from what growers called 'splitting', that is to say, the flower spike drops at an early stage as a result of the stalk breaking.

Among the pale blue cultivars 'Perle Brillante' is the one most often cultivated.

Hyacinthus 'Pink Pearl'

Hyacinthus 'Hollyhock'

HYACINTHUS HYBRID – PINK

Hyacinths are excellent for bedding and are frequently used for this purpose. Size 16–17 cm (6½–7 in.) bulbs are particularly useful; 60–70 bulbs may be planted per square metre (yard) at a depth of 10–12 cm (4–5 in.). They can be planted at any time during October and November, or even at the beginning of December. Combination with daisies or forget-me-nots gives a pleasing effect and at the same time prolongs the flowering period of the bed.

'Marconi' (dark pink) has finer spikes than 'Pink Pearl' illustrated above. 'Lady Derby' (the spikes are somewhat meagre), 'Queen of the Pinks' and 'Anna Marie' are other excellent races in this group.

HYACINTHUS HYBRID – DOUBLE-FLOWERED

The group of double-flowered hyacinths is small and they are not cultivated on a large scale. Only a few growers are able to supply them. Nevertheless I thought it would be amusing to mention them in this book, if only because of their one-time importance. In the years 1733–1736 prices of 500–600 Dutch florins (1 florin is approximately 16p) were paid for hyacinth bulbs, especially for the double-flowered forms. At that time the hyacinth was fashionable and every rich man wished to possess them. Nowadays double-flowered hyacinths are available in white, pink and red and other colours. The use of hyacinths in borders and beds has been discussed previously. However, they can also successfully be planted in window-boxes and on balconies, provided they are treated with extra care during periods of severe frost.

Ipheion uniflorum

Iris bakeriana

IPHEION UNIFLORUM (Spring starflower)

You may have difficulty in finding the little bulbs under this name; it should therefore be mentioned that they are also marketed under the names of Brodiaea and Triteleia.

The flowers, one to each 15—20 cm (6—8 in.) tall stem, which explains the name 'uniflorum', appear in April and May.

We plant them in October at a depth of 6—7 cm (2½—3in.). They are winter-hardy, although they are natives of Peru and Argentina. This cheerful and profusely flowering little plant demands plenty of sun. If left undisturbed for several years, it will flower in increasing abundance.

IRIS BAKERIANA

Every book, including this one, has its limitations. In mentioning this particular species of iris it is therefore intended to honour at the same time all other, less well-known species of the genus. Their number is legion. To mention but a few: the yellow and white I. bucharica, which grows to 35 cm (14 in.) and flowers in late April; the beautiful I. hoogiana with its lavender-coloured flowers in May; and we should not forget the pale mauve I. magnifica, which grows to 40 cm (16 in.). And consider the strange colouring of I. tuberosa (green with dark brown), sometimes also called Hermodactylus tuberosus.

To come back to I. bakeriana.

This is counted among dwarf irises, 15 cm (6 in.) and, like the others, flowers very early (February—March). The species occurs wild in Mesopotamia and elsewhere.

Time and depths of planting, etc. are similar to those of I. reticulata and others.

Iris danfordiae

Iris histrioides 'Major'

IRIS DANFORDIAE

The low-growing, early-flowering iris species, such as I. dandordiae illustrated above, are among the bulbous flowers I love best. Mother nature has equipped them with every possible advantage. The warm yellow, beautifully shaped flowers, as well as the fact that the leaves are practically absent at the time of flowering, are but a few. Add to these the early flowering season (in mild winters late February) and you have perfection.

Again Asia Minor is the country of origin. What a lot of beautiful bulbous plants have come to us from this region! The fine whitish bulbs of this species are thin and sharply pointed.

IRIS HISTRIOIDES

The flowering period of this species is also February or March. It is often the 'Major' variety which is cultivated; it is somewhat larger in its parts than the species itself which has bright violet-blue flowers. Again (cf. I. danfordiae and I. bakeriana), Asia Minor is the country of origin. All the dwarf irises mentioned here must be planted in October at a depth of 6 cm ($2\frac{1}{2}$ in.).

They can be used in many different ways: in the rock-garden, in front of a border or in a sheltered spot against a south-facing wall or fence to bring them into flower earlier.

Make sure, however, that you always plant them in large clumps (possibly in large flower pots) — at least ten to a clump and only 4 cm (2 in.) apart.

Iris hybrid 'Golden Harvest'

Iris reticulata

IRIS HYBRID (Dutch iris)

Dutch irises are not very suitable for garden use, among other reasons because the flowering period is short, the plants collapse readily and the foliage becomes unsightly immediately after flowering. Nevertheless they deserve a place in this book, if only because of the beauty of the flowers.

It is for that reason also that quite a lot of people accept the less favourable characteristics into the bargain, and plant in a group in the border. However, they are more often grown in a special corner reserved for flowers for cutting.

They are planted in October in an open, sunny place at a depth of 8 cm ($3\frac{1}{2}$ in.). They flower mid-June to early July in the colours blue, white, yellow and violet. Average height is 60 cm (2 ft).

IRIS RETICULATA

This species grows wild in the Caucasus. A fair number of cultivars are known. Not that the original, which is of a deep violet, is not a fine specimen — on the contrary; but the variety available provides us with more opportunities.

The cultivar 'Cantab' is pale blue with orange blotches; 'J. S. Dijt', on the other hand, has purple flowers, fragrant like the others. 'Harmony' is of an even blue, while 'Pauline', has violet-purple flowers. Flowering is in March. Once the flowers have died down, the foliage continues to grow. Leave this foliage as long as possible, for it is in this period that the bulbs develop most. When the foliage has died down, lift bulbs and store for subsequent use.

Iris xiphioides

Ixia hybrids

IRIS XIPHIOIDES (English iris)

Although I would not recommend English irises for use in the border any more than I would the Dutch species, they nevertheless deserve mention because of their good cutting properties — provided, that is, they are cut while still in bud.

If, therefore, you have a corner reserved for flowers for cutting, you should plant some of these English irises, which are usually sold in a mixture of colours.

The name English iris is somewhat misleading, for the plants originate in the mountain meadows of the Pyrenees. Perhaps they were noticed first in English gardens and thus received their name. Compared to most other iris species they flower fairly late, namely in June–July. They grow to $\pm$ 60 cm (2 ft).

IXIA HYBRID

If you find it difficult, or even impossible, to resist the temptation to pick flowers in your garden, you should plant some ixia corms.

Choose a sunny spot, which must on no account be waterlogged in winter. Plant the corms at a depth of 6–7 cm ($2\frac{1}{2}$–3 in.) in the last week of November or the first week of December and cover them with a thick layer of straw, bracken, peat, ashes or leaves, for this little South African plant does not tolerate frost. When there is no longer any danger of frost, we remove the covering; in June they will flower profusely. Cut a few stems; they keep very well in water. Ixia, which grows to around 30–40 cm (12–16 in.) can also be used in the border.

Ixiolirion montanum

Leucojum vernum

IXIOLIRION MONTANUM

This fine plant (syn. Ixiolirion pallasii, I. tataricum) flowers in June, when few other bulbous plants are in flower and most summer-flowering perennials are not yet at their best. It is therefore a useful plant for the perennial border, providing a little colour in June.

We plant in October at a depth of 6–7 cm (2½–3 in.). The plant occurs wild in the Caucasus, in Asia and elsewhere, and grows to $\pm$ 40 cm (16 in.).

Rich, deeply dug, well-drained soil, reducing the chance of waterlogging in winter to a minimum, and a sunny situation, are essential, otherwise do not plant before March.

Light covering in winter is advised, if they are to be left in the ground. Towards the end of July, or whenever the leaves have died down, the bulbs are lifted and stored dry until they can be planted again.

LEUCOJUM VERNUM (Snowflake)

To naturalise leucojums they should preferably be planted under smaller trees or under shrubs, as well as in the lawn. On superficial acquaintance the flowers remind us somewhat of snowdrops. However, the six petals of the leucojum are of equal length, whereas in the snowdrop the three inner ones are considerably shorter.

The spring snowflake, a rare native of Britain, flowers in March–April; it usually has one (rarely two) drooping flowers to each 15–20 cm (6–8 in.) tall stem. Another pretty native is the summer snowflake (L. aestivum), which grows to as much as 50 cm (20 in.) and flowers in May–June. This plant likes a slightly damp position. Leucojum is planted in October at a depth of 6–8 cm (2½–3½ in.).

Lilium candidum

Lilium henryi

LILIUM CANDIDUM (Madonna lily)

First grown in monastic gardens, this beautiful and easily-grown lily soon spread to cottage gardens, where in England it has been grown for more than 500 years. Its native habitat is held to be the Caucasus, but it also grows wild in several parts of Southern Europe.

The fragrant flowers come out in June; the stems are up to 100 cm ($3\frac{1}{2}$ ft) tall. In the case of lilies it is unusual, when indicating planting depth, to give the thickness of soil between the upper part of the bulb and the surface. Lilium candidum is planted in September with its top only $\pm$ 3 cm ($1\frac{1}{2}$ in.) below the soil.

LILIUM HENRYI

This truly magnificent lily species was discovered towards the end of the last century by Dr. Henry, who found it growing among shrubs on chalky rocks in Central China. The plants are consequently grateful for chalky soil and light shade. Ground cover is also advisable. I would recommend planting the bulbs at a depth of 8–10 cm (3–4 in.) among ground-covering plants such as, for instance, vincas (periwinkle) pachysandra or sweet-scented woodruff. This lily is usually planted in spring but may be planted from October onwards, if wished. It flowers late (August–September). It is one of the tallest lilies in the garden and easily reaches a height of 150 cm (5 ft.) It is important – and this applies to all lilies – to make sure that the roots are healthy and moist and not desiccated; if they are dry, the bulb is unlikely to grow.

Lilium hybrid 'Midcentury'

Lilium pumilum

LILIUM HYBRID

These 'Midcentury' hybrids were developed by Messrs. Jan de Graaff of Oregon (United States). Their calices are erect and they are available in the colours orange, red, yellow and orangy-yellow. They reach an average height of 75 cm (30 in.) and flower in June. These lilies greatly resemble the so-called Lilium umbellatum which is the result of crossing L. bulbi ferum (Alps) and L. maculatum, the latter itself being the result of crossing.

The correct name is L. hollandicum, but they are better known as L. umbellatum. Rich, well-drained soil is essential, not only for these species, but for all other lilies as well.

L. umbellatum, usually orange or red, flowers in June or July. Like the hybrids, it may be left undisturbed for many years. Its height is 60–80 cm (24–32 in.).

LILIUM PUMILUM

There are over 100 lily species growing wild in the Northern Hemisphere. Lilium pumilum (syn. L. tenuifolium) is found in Siberia and Korea. Although clay or loamy soil is most suitable, they will grow in other kinds of soil as well. They are planted in November at a depth of 3–4 cm ($1\frac{1}{4}$–$1\frac{3}{4}$ in.). The beautiful drooping flowers come out in June and July; the stems grow to 50–60 cm (20–24 in.).

Another form, L. speciosum 'Rubrum', which comes from Japan, is of importance chiefly for cutting purposes, but it may also be used in the border. We plant these in spring at a depth of 8–10 cm (3–4 in.). They may be left in the ground, provided they are protected in winter. The pendulous flowers, which are carmine-pink with white and numerous carmine blotches, appear in July–August. Maximum height 100 cm ($3\frac{1}{2}$ ft).

Lilium regale

Lilium tigrinum

LILIUM REGALE

Everyone appears to like lilies; nevertheless we rarely see them used in gardens, which is unfortunate. It is true that they are more demanding than, for instance, daffodils or tulips. But just think what you get in return! Lilium regale comes from Western China and was not brought to Western Europe until this century. This species flowers profusely (in July), especially when it is left undisturbed for several years (light covering essential). The bulbs are supplied in spring and should be planted immediately at a depth of 8 cm (3 in.). Another fine form is the Golden-rayed Lily of Japan, L. auratum. Lime-free soil and a cool situation should be provided. The bulbs are planted in spring at a depth of 8 cm (3 in.). This tall lily, it grows to ± 150 cm (5 ft) has white-speckled flowers with yellow bands on the inside of the petals.

LILIUM TIGRINUM (Tiger-lily)

Tiger-lilies are among the most easily grown lilies. They flower in August or September, and look well in a mixed border of perennials, for instance in combination with plants such as Salvia superba (which has a deep purple inflorescence). Tiger-lilies are usually planted in early spring, but this can also be done in the autumn. They are planted 20 cm (8 in.) apart at a depth of 8–10 cm (3–4 in.). This tall lily grows tp ± 150 cm (5 ft) and tolerates sun as well as partial shade. Several races are in cultivation. A very fine specimen is L. martagon. The wine-red flowers, thickly speckled with dark red, grow in a raceme of up to 12 flowers per stem. They appear in June and July.

The height of this species, which grows wild in the Alps and elsewhere, is ± 125 cm ($4\frac{1}{2}$ ft).

Muscari armeniacum

Muscari botryoides 'Album'

MUSCARI ARMENIACUM (Grape hyacinth)

This well-known and well-loved little bulbous plant can be used in numerous ways. Every year I never fail to be impressed by the manner in which they have been used in bulb displays, such as in the gardens at Keukenhof, Holland. You may have seen the vistas among the trees yourself, where thousands of them appear to form a deep blue carpet. Grape hyacinths can also be naturalised in clumps and occasionally we see them planted in beds under much taller narcissi, or anywhere in the border. They can also be forced indoors.

And as if that were not enough, they are also suitable for cutting and can be obtained from florists.

MUSCARI BOTRYOIDES

Muscari botryoides 'Album' is a white grape hyacinth. The ordinary blue species is cultivated as well, and it is to this that the plant owes its common name, for botryoides means 'grape-like'.

The bulbs of the various muscari species are planted in October–November at a depth of 6–7 cm ($\pm$ 2½ in.), 7 cm (2½ in.) apart. They have the great advantage that, although they have come from rather warmer climates, they can survive the winter without protection. There is one species, in fact, M. racemosum, which is occasionally found wild in the east of Britain.

Lovers of bees might like to know that the flowers are generous hosts to these industrious nectar-collectors.

Muscari comosum 'Plumosum'

Narcissus cyclamineus 'Peeping Tom'

MUSCARI COMOSUM

This species grows wild in Mediterranean countries and in the Canary Islands. The common form, which hardly resembles the grape hyacinth, has fertile (greenish) flowers, as well as infertile purple ones which form the upper part of the raceme. In the 'Plumosum' (monstrosum) form illustrated above, the actual flowers are usually absent. Its decorative value lies in the violet-coloured, strongly and irregularly ramified flower-stems, which give it the common name of the Feather hyacinth. Apart from the species illustrated, numerous other species and cultivars may be mentioned. A cultivar which is currently very popular is 'Blue Spike' of the species armeniacum, which has double blue flowers. M. tubergenianum, from Iran, whose racemes consist of pale and dark blue florets, is also well worth growing.

NARCISSUS CYCLAMINEUS

A close friend of mine has carefully studied the development of bulbs of Narcissus cyclamineus 'February Gold' planted in 1969 and since left undisturbed. Every year he counts the number of flowers produced and by 1973 this number was still increasing — clear evidence of their suitability for naturalisation.

'Peeping Tom' has a longer trumpet than 'February Gold' and the flowers also emerge further from the foliage. Apart from this the two cultivars are much alike. Personally I am very fond of 'Dove Wings', which also flowers early and for a long time, and which has white petals and primrose yellow trumpets.

The important characteristic of this group is the fact that the petals are sharply reflexed.

Narcissus (trumpet) 'Mount Hood'

Narcissus (trumpet) 'Magnet'

NARCISSUS – TRUMPET DAFFODIL GROUP

Most of the narcissi we plant in our dardens are hybrids of wild species. Unlike the tulip and the hyacinth, interest in narcissi did not get under way until the beginning of this century. Whereas tulips (17th century) and hyacinths (18th century) had long been popular, narcissus were only generally planted in the latter half of the 19th century, when a great deal of hybridisation was carried out by amateurs.

Interest in these flowers was small until then, and was chiefly concentrated on the many-flowered narcissi. Nowadays trumpet narcissi, like those illustrated above, form the most important group. A daffodil belongs to the trumpet group if the trumpet is of equal length or longer than the petals. Such plants have only one flower to a stem. They are very useful in the garden as well as for cutting. Trumpet daffodils are subdivided into yellow, bi-coloured and white forms, the yellow types being by far the most often used.

'Golden' Harvest', 'Unsurpassable', 'Rembrandt' and the slightly shorter 'Dutch Master' are the chief cultivars. White trumpet daffodils are no less valuable, although they are rarely used. Apart from 'Mount Hood' which has a prolonged flowering season and has strikingly wide petals, the slightly earlier flowering 'Beersheba' should be mentioned. Both grow to about 40–50 cm (16–20 in.). 'Magnet' is currently the most popular bi-coloured trumpet daffodil, with a cream-yellow trumpet and white petals. In recent years there has been some demand for so-called pink trumpet daffodils, such as 'Rosy Sunrise'. These have a pure white corona (petals) and a pinkish trumpet, which initially is yellow, but later changes colour. The trumpet daffodil I like best is 'W. P. Milner'. This is a representative of the small rock-garden narcissi, and grows to only 20 cm (8 in.); its small, sulphur-yellow flowers appear in April.

74

Narcissus (large-cupped) 'Carlton'

Narcissus (small-cupped) 'Verger'

NARCISSUS — LARGE-CUPPED

For the purpose of naturalising, where the bulbs are left undisturbed for several years, it is preferable to buy fairly young bulbs, the so-called 'rounds'. Although they may flower somewhat less profusely in the first few years, they will last longer.

To plant bulbs in the lawn, remove pieces of turf, plant the bulbs and replace the turf. As you will have noticed in the photograph, large-cupped narcissi have a somewhat smaller cup than trumpet narcissi. This group, too, contains a large number of good cultivars, for instance 'Carlton' (illustrated), 'Yellow Sun' (yellow), 'Fortune' (golden yellow, orange-red cup), 'Semper Avanti' (white with red cup), 'Flower Record' (cream cup, corona orange), not forgetting 'Mrs R. O. Backhouse', which is classified as pink, having a white corona, and apricot-pink cup.

NARCISSUS — SMALL-CUPPED

These charming small narcissi have only very small cups, but for all that are no less beautiful. Worthwhile cultivars are 'Verger' (see illustration), 'Barrett Browning' (white with an orange cup) and 'Edward Buxton' (pale yellow, clear orange corona). To achieve the best possible result with all narcissi, well-dug soil, rich in humus, is essential. Too much water in winter is fatal. If the soil is very dry, it may be mixed with some peat.

Narcissi can be planted from September to the beginning of December. Late September–early October seems to be the best time. Planting depth is 15 cm (6 in.); distance between bulbs varies between 10 and 20 cm (4 and 8 in.).

I suggest you plant some bulbs in a special corner for cutting purposes.

Narcissus (double) 'Van Sion'

Narcissus (double) 'Cheerfulness'

NARCISSUS – DOUBLE

The history of the double narcissus illustrated above goes back several centuries. In a book by the Dutch author, J. B. Janse, called *In Geuren en Kleuren* I discovered that a certain Vincent Sion, a Fleming living in London, cultivated this variety as early as the 17th century. Its true name is therefore V. Sion, which later erroneously became 'Van Sion'. It also has the synonym N. telamonius plenus.

As the flowerheads are heavy, a sheltered position is indicated, for they cannot withstand strong winds.

'Texas' has yellow flowers with an orange centre, and 'Mary Copeland' is white, with an orange-red centre. Both these are also useful in the garden.

NARCISSUS – DOUBLE MANY-FLOWERED

Both ordinary as well as many-flowered narcissi are nowadays classified under the double group. In general the latter is valued most. The white cultivar 'Cheerfulness' grows to about 50 cm (20 in.); flowers fairly late (early May) and is very fragrant.

The soft yellow 'Yellow Cheerfulness' is found less and less frequently. 'Bridal Crown' (creamy white) is a newer cultivar.

Since narcissi are usually left undisturbed for several years running, the storage of the bulbs does not play such an important part. However, when it is necessary to store them temporarily, this raises few problems, for they may be kept out of doors, provided they never get wet.

Narcissus jonquilla, 'Trevithian'

Narcissus (tazetta) 'Geranium'

NARCISSUS – JONQUILS AND PSEUDONARCISSUS

Although the 'Trevithian' cultivar illustrated above is not a true botanical narcissus, both these kinds nevertheless lead us to the fairyland of wild narcissi, where we find so much beauty. Try the smallest of all, once rightly called N. minimus, but now renamed N. asturiensis; or the little N. nanus, classified as the earliest flowering of all, and marketed under the name Narcissus lobularis. Its height is 15 cm (6 in.) and its colour yellow and white, the trumpet being the yellow part.

Jonquil narcissi are rush-leaved and strongly scented. The ordinary species, also a dwarf, grows to 20–30 cm (8–12 in.). 'Trevithian' may grow to as much as 35 cm (14 in.).

Needless to say the small bulbs of the species are planted at shallow depths 'see also Corbularia bulbocodium).

NARCISSUS TAZETTA

There are not many true tazetta narcissi left. The only variety belonging to this group is the so-called 'Paperwhite', which can be brought to flower so early indoors, and of which the bulbs are imported from France. Most cultivars are the result of crossing the species poeticus and tazetta.

The narcissi belonging to the latter group have 4–12 flowers to each stem. Light covering in winter is desirable, for they are more sensitive to frost than, for instance, the trumpet narcissi. 'Cragford' is an earlier-flowering variety than 'Geranium'. The former, often used for growing in pots, has white flowers with an orange cup. Other varieties of importance are 'L'Innocence' (white with a pale yellow cup) and 'Laurens Koster' (white perianth and yellow corona).

Narcissus triandrus 'Thalia'

Ornithogalum nutans

NARCISSUS TRIANDRUS

The cultivar 'Thalia' illustrated above is becoming less popular. Nevertheless it is a good example of the group to which it belongs. It is a low-growing narcissus, particularly suitable for growing in the rock-garden. It flowers comparatively late, namely from the end of April into May.

'Thalia' has been supplanted by other very fine forms, for instance 'Tresamble', which has three or more pure white flowers to a stalk, or 'Silver Chimes', 35 cm (14 in.) in height, whose pure white flowers have a small cream-coloured crown. A cultivar with the name 'April Tears' (they must surely be tears of joy) has yellow drooping flowers, and is the shortest, to 17 cm (7 in.) in height. 'Liberty Bells', finally, produces two to four soft yellow flowers per stalk.

ORNITHOGALUM NUTANS (Drooping Star of Bethlehem)

Floras refer to the drooping Star of Bethlehem as a (fairly) rare plant, occurring in meadows and woodland. It is probable that it has naturalised here from introductions, for elsewhere its native habitat is given as the Balkans and Asia Minor.

Anyhow, the species may be used to good purpose in our gardens, in the first place for naturalising in suitable places, but also in the border. The racemes consist of about ten flowers, all pointing one way; the height of the stems is about 40 cm (16 in.).

The plant is perfectly hardy and flowers in April or May.

The photograph above was taken in the School of Botany in Leyden, Holland, where a large group has been planted under an enormous Ginkgo biloba tree, which has been there since 1785.

Ornithogalum thyrsoides   *Ornithogalum umbellatum*

ORNITHOGALUM THYRSOIDES (Chincherinchee)

This species, whose infloresence is a heavy pyramid-shaped spike, is of importance chiefly for cutting. For this purpose they are grown under glass as well as out of doors.

In water they last longer than practically any other flower. It is regrettable that the flowers are dyed all sorts of colours.

Very occasionally we see this South African plant used in the garden (in full sunlight), and in a warm, sheltered border, with protection in winter.

The plants are by no means hardy. We plant towards the end of April at a depth of 6—8 cm ($2\frac{1}{2}$—$3\frac{1}{2}$ in.). They flower in summer and reach a height of around 40 cm (15 in.).

As the foliage is not very beautiful, the plants easily give an untidy effect to the border.

ORNITHOGALUM UMBELLATUM (Star of Bethlehem)

The name Star of Bethlehem is very confusing, for it is also the name of the well-known indoor plant Campanula isophylla 'Alba', with which it has nothing in common, apart from the colour of the flowers.

This is another species which we very occasionally encounter in partially shady spots in the countryside. The flowers are arranged in loose umbels. They appear a little later than those of the drooping Star of Bethlehem (May—June). Height is 20—25 cm (8—10 in.).

On fine sunny days the star-shaped flowers open wide, but on cool grey days they remain closed.

Both species (O. nutans as well) are planted in October at a depth of 8—10 cm (3—4 in.).

Oxalis adenophylla

Polygonatum multiflorum

OXALIS ADENOPHYLLA (Wood sorrel)

Few plants, especially bulbous and tumerous plants, are of ornamental value when not in flower. Oxalis adenophylla, a native of South America, is an exception, for its blue-green foliage is very decorative.

Moreover, it grows profusely in May–June and has pretty flowers. It is an excellent plant for the rock-garden, where it must be given a sunny position. It is also grown in pots for use indoors.

The strangely shaped bulbs (they look like balls of coarse string) are planted in October at a depth of 6–7 cm (2½–3 in.). They may be left in the ground for several years. They grow to only 10 cm (4 in.).

Of the other species I shall mention only O. deppei, which is pinky-red and should be planted in spring. It has a prolonged flowering season.

POLYGONATUM MULTIFLORUM (Solomon's seal)

This plant owes its English name to the scars left on the thick rootstock by the previous year's flower-stems. Solomon's seal is neither a bulbous nor a tuberous plant; it has rhizomes, and is sometimes classified among perennials.

There is a slow-growing species, P. odoratum, which grows wild in woodlands on chalky soil; this has only one or two flowers in each axil. The ordinary Solomon's seal, on the other hand, has several flowers placed in racemes.

The plant grows to 50–100 cm (20–40 in.) depending on soil and situation. The flowering period is May–June. Plant in autumn at a depth of 10 cm (4 in.), in a shady position.

80

Puschkinia scilloides

Ranunculus asiaticus

PUSCHKINIA SCILLOIDES

Here is another valuable 'wild' flower. 'Wild' is not the right word, for it will never become a nuisance. The fact that it spreads constantly and new plants grow both from the older bulbs and from seed, can only fill us with gratitude. We plant them in October at a depth of 5–6 cm (2–2½ in.) in places where they are welcome to spread. They will flourish in the most unfavourable positions, for instance under trees. The almost pure white flowers, with their characteristic blue stripe down the petals, appear in April. Some people consider it a disadvantage that the flower-stems – 15 to 20 cm (6–8 in.) – are hardly taller than the leaves, but every plant after all has its advantages and disadvantages.

RANUNCULUS ASIATICUS

We distinguish between several different groups of ranunculi, namely Turkish (Turban), French, Persian and Peony-flowered strains. Differences are slight and need not concern us here, though it is important to mention that the Turkish ranunculi can be planted October–November, and the others around February.

They should be planted, claw side downwards, at a depth of no more than 2–3 cm (1–1½ in.). Having been planted early, the Turkish ranunculi flower from the end of April onwards; the others flower in June. Ranunculi grow to 25–50 cm (8–10 in.) and often have double or semi-double flowers in a variety of colours. They are used mainly in the border. After the leaves have turned yellow and the flowers are faded, the tubers should be lifted, dried and stored in a cool dry place until planting time. Ranunculi are also excellent for cutting. They prefer moisture-retaining rich soil and a sunny position.

Sauromatum venosum

Scilla hispanica

SAUROMATUM VENOSUM

This plant is better known by the name Arum cornutum or Sauromatum guttatum.

It is fairly well known as a tuber which can be brought to flower indoors without soil or water. It will flower if just placed dry on the windowsill in spring. However, both the flower and the bract have a disagreeable smell, so perhaps it would be better to put it in the garden, where the unpleasant scent will not worry you. After it has flowered without foliage, beautifully shaped leaves on speckled stems are developed. Normally they are planted out of doors in spring. Rich soil is indicated.

The correct depth of planting of this native of the Himalayas is $\pm$ 8 cm (3 in.).

SCILLA HISPANICA (Spanish squill)

In its wild form this native of Spain and Portugal has violet-blue flowers, but in the course of time numerous cultivars have been produced with larger flowers and of different colours (white, pink, pale and dark blue).

This species, now more correctly, though less commonly, called Endymion hispanicus (syn. Scilla campanulata), differs from other well-known scilla species, such as S. sibirica, both in its flowering season (May) and its height, to 50 cm (20 in.).

We plant in October at a depth of $\pm$ 8 cm (3 in.) and $\pm$ 12 cm (5 in.) apart. Deeply dug soil, supplies with well-rotted manure, is best. Light covering in winter is to be recommended. Did you know, by the way, that there is also a scilla which can be grown as an indoor plant? This is S. violacea, which originates in South Africa and has beautifully marked foliage and greenish flowers.

Scilla non-scripta

Scilla sibirica

SCILLA NON-SCRIPTA (Bluebell)

This is the well-known and much eulogized bluebell which grows wild in Britain. Endymion non-scriptus is its correct name, though catalogues usually list it under scilla.

This species, less often in cultivation than S. hispanica, is lower growing than the latter and has narrower leaves and somewhat smaller and narrower flowers. The flowers are, moreover, placed on one side of the raceme only. This bluebell can be warmly recommended for naturalising. Its height when in flower (in May) is only 15—20 cm (6—8 in.).

There are cultivars of this scilla as well, e.g. 'Alba' (white) and 'Carnea' (pink).

SCILLA SIBIRICA (Siberian squill)

This is one of the scilla species most often cultivated in Britain. Obvious reasons are its early and profuse flowering and the fact that it is easy to grow. It may be used in several places, such as the rock-garden, the border and under trees.

It flowers as early as March, at the same time as crocuses and other early birds. Its height is only 10 cm (4 in.).

This does not apply to the large-flowering selection 'Spring Beauty', which grows to 15 cm (6 in.) and has firmer stems.

Another beautiful form is S. bifolia, which has clusters of violet-blue fragrant flowers.

The early-flowering scillas are planted in September—October at a depth of 5—7 cm (2—3 in.).

Scilla tubergeniana

Sparaxis tricolor

SCILLA TUBERGENIANA

In mild winters this scilla species may flower as early as the end of February; it is the earliest-flowering of all the species.

The other scilla species described here have been cultivated ever since the 16th, 17th or 18th century, but S. tubergeniana was not imported into Holland from Northern Persia by Messrs. Tubergen until as late as 1931, in which year it also reached Britain. It was a very valuable introduction, not only because it flowers so early, but also because of its white and soft china-blue flowers.

In addition to this fine species I should like to mention S. pratensis, listed in catalogues as S. amethystina, which flowers in late May but is rarely used. The small blue flowers grow in pyramid-shaped spikes.

SPARAXIS TRICOLOR

This is a cormous plant belonging to the family of Iridaceae. It is of South African origin and prefers a sunny position in the border. The comparatively small corms dislike too much water in winter, so pick a dry spot.

When planted any time from September to December, at a depth of around 7 cm (3 in.) they must be well covered. A 15 cm (6 in.) thick layer of leaves, bracken or straw is in a severe winter no superfluous luxury.

After flowering, around June, the foliage quickly goes off. When the leaves have died down the corms may be lifted and stored in a dry, warm place until they can be planted again. The plant's height is around 35 cm (14 in.).

Sprekelia formosissima

Tigridia pavonia

SPREKELIA FORMOSISSIMA (Jacobean lily)

This is by no means an easy plant to grow. It is closely related to the amaryllis or, to name it correctly, to hippeastrum. It is very much a plant for a knowledgeable botanist. You might try it, and if you are successful you may count yourself among this category.

Plant the bulbs, which come from Mexico, in April in a sunny and sheltered position, and make sure the soil is well nourished and deeply dug. Depth of planting should be 6–8 cm (2–3 in.).

The magnificent flowers appear in June, almost at the same time as the foliage. The plant grows to about 30 cm (12 in.) tall.

The bulbs are lifted in early October and stored in a warm, dry place at a maximum temperature of 20° C (68° F). In really warm gardens it can be left out of doors all year, but should have some protection from rain and frost.

TIGRIDIA PAVONIA (Tiger flower)

I must confess that I have not often been entirely successful with this exceptionally fine cormous plant, even though I have always followed instructions to the letter. I pass these on in the hope that you will have better results (in the shape of truly magnificently shaped and coloured flowers) than I did.

Provide rich and moisture-retaining soil and a sunny position. Plant the corms around the end of April at a depth of 7–8 cm (3–3½ in.).

The flowers, each of which last only one day, come out from July to September. The plant grows to 40–50 cm (16–20 in.). Some time after flowering the corms are usually lifted to be stored cool and dry during the winter, but in warm gardens in the south and west it is possible to leave them in the ground over winter.

Triteleia laxa

Tulipa (S.E.T.) 'Couleur Cardinal'

TRITELEIA LAXA

This lily-like little plant grows wild in California, which implies that it is not hardy in severe winters or cold gardens. It is therefore advisable to protect it in winter, preferably not with peat, but with bracken, straw or leaves. Fir branches are also useful for this purpose. Peat looks much tidier, but does not provide much insulation.

Triteleia, often still called Brodiaea, is planted in November at a depth of 6–8 cm (2–3 in.). They like a really sunny place.

The flowers appear in June; the height of the plant is 50 cm (20 in.). It is advisable to lift the corms in August and replant them after a period of rest, if the summer is cool and wet.

TULIPA – SINGLE EARLY TULIP

'Early singles' form one of the many groups into which tulips are divided according to the international Classified List.

Early single tulips are particularly suitable for garden use, since they are relatively low-growing, ± 30–40 cm (12–16 in.) and have firm stems. Compared to those of various other groups the flowers are fairly small.

Flowering starts about the middle of April.

A number of early single tulips, as well as early doubles, are frequently used in beds. 60–80 bulbs are planted per square metre (square yard). Good cultivars are: 'Bellona' (a pure yellow), 'Couleur Cardinal' (see illustration), 'Brilliant Star' (the well-known red Christmas tulip), 'General de Wet' (orange, fragrant), 'Keizerskroon' (scarlet edged with yellow) and 'Christmas Marvel' (cherry red).

Tulipa (D.E.T.) 'Mr. v.d. Hoef'

Tulipa (Darwin-hybrid) 'Apeldoorn'

TULIPA – DOUBLE EARLY TULIP

Double early tulips are particularly recommended for bedding. The double flowers and dense planting, 80–100 bulbs per square metre (square yard) produce a rich colour effect. Since nearly all the cultivars in this group have been developed by mutation from the pink 'Murillo' see the chapter on the production of new varieties, p. 13), both height, ± 30 cm (12 in.) and flowering season (second half of April) are uniform. They can therefore be planted in a mixture of colours.

Recommended varieties are: 'Mr. v. d. Hoef' (see illustration), 'Orange Nassau' (orange-red), 'Peach Blossom' (deep pink), 'Marechal Niel' (yellow flushed with orange), 'Schoonoord' (white) and 'Willemsoord' (carmine red, white-edged). 'Carlton' (red) is also good, but has not been produced from 'Murillo' and has taller stems.

TULIPA – DARWIN HYBRIDS

This group has gained enormously in popularity in the last twenty years or so. The tulips were developed in Holland (by Messrs. D. W. Lefeber & Co. of Lisse) by crossing Darwin tulips and Tulipa fosteriana. They are prime growers, producing large, often red, flowers. They flower in late April–early May; their stems are 60–70 cm (24–28 in.) tall. They are much in demand for growing in the garden, but are also marketed on a large scale as cut flowers.

One of the best known is 'Apeldoorn' (see illustration). Another fine variety is 'Golden Apeldoorn' (yellow). 'Oxford' is an orange-red with a large yellow base. 'Gudoshnik' (what a name!) has deep yellow flowers, flecked and striped with apricot. 'Diplomate' (red), finally, flowers a little later and has more pointed petals.

Tulipa (Triumph) 'Paul Richter'

Tulipa (Mendel) 'Olga'

TULIPA — TRIUMPH

Triumph tulips were developed by crossing single early and mainly Darwin tulips. They possess excellent properties as garden tulips, but also for forcing under glass to be marketed as cut flowers.

Together with the Darwin tulips they are the most important group. They have firm stems, flower in May and grow to 50—60 cm (20—24 in.). Of the many excellent kinds in this group I shall only mention a few: 'Lustige Witwe' (red, white-edged), 'Prominence' (dark red), 'Paris' (orange-red with a yellow edge), 'Preludium' (pink), 'Levant' (yellow), 'Kees Nelis' (red with yellow edge), 'Paul Richter' (see illustration), 'Emmy Peeck' (lilac-pink), and 'Mirjoran' (carmine red, cream-edged).

TULIPA — MENDEL

Mendel tulips are the result of crossing Darwin varieties and Duc van Tol tulips. The latter are nowadays rarely cultivated; they used to be marketed as Christmas tulips. Duc van Tol tulips grow to only 15 cm (6 in.) and flower in early April.

Mendel tulips are not very suitable for the garden, as many kinds have rather limp stems. Specialists consider 'Krelage's Triumph' (purply-red) and 'Pink Trophy' (salmon-pink) to be the best. The flowering season is around the end of April; they grow to 40—50 cm (16—20 in.). Some other races which might be used as 'Olga' (see illustration), 'Athleet. (white), 'Orange Wonder' (bronzy orange with red shading) and 'Golden Olga' (red, yellow-edged).

Tulipa (Darwin) 'Rose Copeland'

Tulipa (Darwin) 'Cordell Hull'

TULIPA — DARWIN

Darwin tulips were developed in Flanders, Belgium, and introduced for sale by Messrs. Krelage & Son around 1890. Their origin is somewhat obscure. In the thirties Darwin tulips formed the most important group, but later they were supplanted by others, such as Triumph and Darwin hybrids. Darwin tulips have tall, generally fairly firm stems, 60—80 cm (24—30 in.). The flowers are usually fairly large, oval-shaped and broad-based. They flower in May. It is remarkable that, in spite of the fact that out of doors they flower late, they can easily be forced. 'Rose Copeland' (see illustration), 'Zwanenburg' (white), 'Sunkist' (yellow), 'Gander' (deep pink) and 'Pink Supreme' (pink) are very useful strains. If you like something unusual, you should choose the so-called black tulip 'Queen of Night' (the darkest tulip of all). 'Cordell Hull' (illustration) and 'Montgomery' (white, red-edged) are remarkable forms. The two latter cultivars used to be classified among broken or Rembrandt tulips, but nowadays they are counted among the Darwin tulips.

They may be planted from mid-October up till Christmas.

Very early planting has the disadvantage that they emerge from the ground too soon and risk damage to the shoots. On the other hand if we postpone planting too long, early frosts may play us false. Depth of planting is 8—10 cm (3—4 in.); planting distance varies between 10 and 15 cm (4 and 6 in.) depending on the strain. Tulips are winter-hardy. They are sometimes given protection, but this is not essential.

Tulipa (lily-flowered) 'Aladdin'

Tulipa (S.L.T.) 'Mrs. John Scheepers'

TULIPA – LILY-FLOWERED

If you have visited the Keukenhof in Lisse, in the Netherlands, you will doubtless have been impressed by the enormous number of cultivars found there. The official classification contains 3,000 of which, I am told, about 2,000 are still in cultivation, although only about 100 occupy more than 10 hectares (25 acres).

In the greenhouses of places like Springfields and the Keukenhof we often encounter graceful lily-flowered tulips. This form will also flourish outside, but prefers a somewhat sheltered position, for the 50–60 cm (20–24 in.) tall stems are none too firm. They flower in late May. Good strains are: 'Aladdin' (see illustration), 'Mariette' (satin-pink), 'West Point' (yellow), 'Queen of Sheba' (red with an orange edge) and 'White Triumphator' (white).

TULIPA – SINGLE LATE TULIP

A number of late-flowering tulips are sometimes called Cottage Tulips, as several of the forms belonging to this group were apparently discovered in old English cottage gardens. The strains in this group show little or no uniformity.

In my opinion, 'Kleurenpracht' should not be missing in any garden. It is yellow with an orange edge and is the last to flower (late May–early June). Fringe-petalled tulips, such as 'Burgundy Lace' (wine red) also belong to the group of single late tulips.

Other important varieties are: 'Mrs John Scheepers' (illustrated), 'Golden Harvest' (yellow), 'Maureen' (white), 'Halcro' (carmine red with a yellow base) and 'Artist' (with very striking rose, yellow and green flowers).

Tulipa (D.L.T.) 'Mount Tacoma'

Tulipa (parrot) 'Black Parrot'

TULIPA – DOUBLE LATE TULIP

I have a confession to make: I don't like late double tulips. In any case I can, with certain exceptions, raise little admiration for double flowers, so that it is understandable that the large double tulips have no attraction to me. However, this is a purely personal opinion and on my numerous visits to the Keukenhof other people's remarks have shown that not everyone agrees with me, and that is just as well. Nevertheless a warning is indicated. Plant them in an airy sheltered position, for their stems are fragile and their flowers are easily bruised. They flower in the second half of May and grow to 40–50 cm (16–20 in.). Some useful strains are: 'Mount Tacoma' (illustrated), 'Eros' (deep pink), 'Livingstone' (red), 'Nizza' (striped red/yellow) and 'Bonanza' (red with a yellow edge). The double late tulips are also sometimes known as the peony flowered tulips.

TULIPA – PARROT

The exotic shape of these flowers, whose petals are often fringed and green-striped, has always appealed to the imagination ot tulip-lovers. The flowers are, moreover, often very large. All this makes the parrot tulip a popular choice for the border.

These tulips have existed for more than 300 years and have 60–70 cm (24–28 in.) tall stems, usually not very firm.

The most interesting forms are: 'Black Parrot' (see illustration), 'Blue Parrot' (clear bronzed violet outside, purple inside), 'Karel Doorman' (cherry red with a yellow edge), 'Fantasy' (pink with green), 'Texas Gold' (yellow with red edge), 'Orange Favorite' (orange with green stripes, fragrant).

Tulipa batalinii

Tulipa eichleri

TULIPA BATALINII

In botanical floras the place of origin of Tulipa batalinii is given as Bokhara. The little bulbs are only 2 cm (1 in.) in diameter and are planted at a depth of 5 cm (2 in.). The creamy yellow flowers appear in late April—early May and reach a height of only 10 cm (4 in.).

'Bronze Charm' has exceptionally beautiful bronze to apricot flowers and is the result of crossing T. batalanii and T. linifolia. It owes the wavy edge of its foliage to the latter. T. linifolia further has small but striking red flowers growing on stalks of 15 cm (6 in.) height. Among the species it is one of the last to flower.

T. urumiensis has star-shaped yellow flowers, 3, 4 or 5 to a stalk.

Finally I must not fail to mention T. celsiana, whose flowers are yellow inside and orange-red outside.

TULIPA EICHLERI

Unlike the bulbs of most other true species, which are very small, the large bulbs of this species are planted to a depth of at least 10 cm (4 in.). It grows to 25 cm (10 in.) and displays its large, bright red flowers at the end of April or the beginning of May.

One beautiful species is the very fragrant T. aucheriana, a native of northern Persia. This grows to less than 10 cm (4 in.); its star-shaped pink flowers appear in April and May.

Tulipa kolpakowskiana grows somewhat taller, 15—20 cm (6—8 in.) and produces golden yellow flowers with wide orange stripes on the outside of the petals.

Tulipa fosteriana 'Red Emperor'

Tulipa greigii 'Oriental Splendour'

TULIPA FOSTERIANA

This is an exceptionally good garden tulip. The large, vividly-coloured flowers and occasionally unusual forms, make them particularly useful for planting in combination with yellow trumpet daffodils, muscari species, such as M. armeniacum 'Blue Spike' and the hyacinths 'Marie' or 'Blue Jacket' (dark blue). Flowering often starts in early April. The best-known cultivar is undoubtedly 'Madame Lefeber', also known under the name 'Red Emperor' (see illustration). Its height is $\pm$ 40 cm (16 in.); the large, beautifully shaped flowers are scarlet. 'Cantata' also has red flowers, but the stems grow to only 25 cm (10 in.). 'Purissima', finally, is a fine white form, growing to 50 cm (20 in.).

Tulipa acuminata, a species with exceptionally narrow pointed yellow and red petals, deserves special mention.

TULIPA GREIGII

The so-called greigii hybrids flower at the end of April—early May. The leaves, which often have wavy margins, are strikingly blotched and streaked with chocolate-magenta. The heights of the different species vary considerably.

'Oriental Splendour', illustrated above, grows to as much as 50 cm (20 in.). The fine cultivar 'Red Riding Hood', one of the greigii hybrids most in demand, does not grow beyond 25 cm (10 in.) and has vivid scarlet flowers. 'Cape Cod' has bronzy-yellow flowers flamed with apricot. Another fine variety is 'Plaisir' (creamy-white, with vermilion red streaks and blotches). 'Zampa', finally, is primrose-yellow with a bronze-green centre and carmine blotches.

Tulipa kaufmanniana 'Stresa'

Tulipa praestans 'Fusilier'

TULIPA KAUFMANNIANA (Waterlily tulip)

The original species, which grows in Turkestan, has creamy-white flowers, carmine red on the outside.

Many strains belong to this species, which is also known by the name Waterlily Tulip. They are short-stemmed, often under 20 cm (8 in.) and have brilliantly coloured flowers. They flower earlier than practically any other tulips, namely from the second half of March onwards. They are particularly suitable for planting in the rock-garden.

The magnificent photograph of 'Stresa' will give you an idea of the beauty of the species. There are others, such as the white and carmine 'The First' and 'Goudstuk' (deep golden yellow, carmine outside). 'Vivaldi', 'Cesar Franck' and 'Johann Strauss' are also very well worth growing.

TULIPA PRAESTANS

The Tulipa praestans 'Fusilier' brings us to the so-called multi-flowered tulips. This form, flowering in mid-April and reaching a height of 25 cm (10 in.) has a number of flowers, varying between 3 and 5, to each stalk. Some firms offer May-flowering multi-flowered tulips, growing to 40—60 cm (16—24 in.). 'Georgette' is yellow with a red edge; 'Orange Bouquet' is orange; 'Monsieur Mottet', finally, has white flowers.

In addition there are the so-called Premul-Bouquet tulips, best ordered from a Dutch bulb specialist. The fact that these tulips, belonging, among others, to the Mendel and Triumph groups, are multi-flowered, is the result of careful selection and cultivation in special temperatures. 'Luzern' (red), 'Turkey' (orange) and 'Prestwick' (pink) can be recommended.

Tulipa tarda

Zephyranthes candida

TULIPA TARDA

There are countless very fine true species tulips in cultivation, rarely bought by the average garden lover. The reason, as always, is: unknown, unloved. Most species at first sight do not look much like tulips, or rather, like the tulips we all know so well.

The species illustrated above, sometimes also called T. dasystemon, grows to only 10 cm (4 in.) and flowers in April. A very fine species is T. turkestanica, white with an orange centre, growing to almost 25 cm (10 in.). For rock-gardens the purple-violet T. violacea can be recommended; this form flowers as early as March; its height is 10 cm (4 in.). Another warmly recommended species is T. clusiana. Its height is 30 cm (12 in.); in April it has white flowers with a cherry-red streak. The small bulbs are planted in October at a depth of 5—6 cm (2—2½ in.).

ZEPHYRANTHES CANDIDA

This bulbous plant belongs to the same family as the narcissus, the snowdrop and the hippeastrum, and comes from Peru. In spite of its southern origin, this striking plant can be grown out of doors. Although practically winter-hardy, a covering of leaves during the winter period is advisable.

The bulbs are planted in spring at a depth of 6—7 cm (2½—3 in.). To achieve a good effect they should be planted at a distance similar to the planting depth. The white flowers come out in summer; their height is only 15 cm (8 in.). The plants require a sheltered position and above all damp, but well-drained, soil.

There is also a yellow cultivar called 'Ajax'.

TABLES AND SURVEYS

1. Border plants

Practically all bulbous and tuberous plants lend themselves for use in the border. Often they are planted among perennials in order to provide colour early in the year. Others, such as lilies, flower in summer and form beautiful combinations with perennials flowering at that time.

Some species (for instance lilies and scilla) can remain in the ground for several years. Others, such as tulips and hyacinths, are planted afresh each autumn and lifted towards summer. Only a few species lend themselves less for use in the border. This is not to say that they cannot be planted there at all, but they are more suitable for other purposes.

Suitable border plants are:

Allium triquetrum	Narcissus asturiensis[2]
— ursinum	— nanus[2]
Anemone nemorosa	Ornithogalum nutans
Convallaria majalis	— umbellatum
Colchicum autumnale[1]	Tulipa aucheriana[3]
Corbularia (Narcissus) bulbocodium[2]	— batalinii
Corydalis cava	— celsiana
— solida	— clusiana
Crocus kotschyanus[1]	— kolpakowskiana
— speciosus[1]	— linifolia
Cyclamen coum	— pulchella
— europaeum	— tarda
Leucojum aestivum	— turkestanica
— vernum	— urumiensis

[1] In autumn they are too insignificant among taller plants.
[2] As their flowers are very small, they need a conspicuous position.
[3] Species tulips should not be allowed to get 'lost' among other plants.

---

2. Bulbs and tubers for naturalisation

This normally means that the bulbs and tubers are left under smaller trees, deciduous shrubs and in grass, without protection in winter. However, the table also contains those bulbs which may be left undisturbed in the border, either with or without protection.

Allium triquetrum[1]	Colchicum-species
— ursinum	Convallaria majalis
Anemone blanda	Corbularia (Narcissus) bulbocodium
— nemorosa	Corydalis-species
Camassia-species	Crocosmia crocosmiiflora
Chionodoxa-species	Crocus-species

Cyclamen-species
Eranthis-species
Eremurus x shelford[2]
Erythronium-species[2]
Fritillaria-species
Galanthus-species
Gladiolus byzantinus
Ipheion uniflorum[2]
Iris bakeriana[3]
— danfordiae[3]
— histrioides[3]
— reticulata[3]

Leucojum-species
Lilium-species
Muscari-species
Narcissus-species[4]
Ornithogalum nutans
— umbellatum
Oxalis adenophylla[2]
Polygonatum-species
Puschkinia scilloides
Scilla-species
Tulipa tarda

[1] Other allium species may also be left in the ground, but in this case foliage often emerges too early and is damaged, making it unsightly in spring.

[2] Need covering in a severe winter.

[3] Are sometimes planted afresh each year.

[4] In most kinds of flowering becomes less profuse after some years.

---

3. Flowers for cutting

The flowers of several species keep fairly well if placed in water indoors. We can, of course, cut the flowers in the border, but this is often a pity. Wherever possible it is better to reserve a special corner for cut flowers.

Allium giganteum
— neapolitanum
— sphaerocephalum
Anemone coronaria
— pavonina
Convallaria majalis
Crocosmia crocosmiiflora
Dahlia hybrid
Eremurus x shelford
Freesia hybrid
Gladiolus hybr. 'Colvillei'
— hybr. 'Gandavensis'

Gladiolus nanus
Iris hybrid (I. hollandica)
Iris xiphioides
Ixia hybrid
Lilium-species[1]
Muscari armeniacum
Narcissus-species[2]
Ornithogalum thyrsoides
Ranunculus asiaticus
Sparaxis tricolor
Tulipa-species[2]

[1] Most lilies are excellent for cutting, but generally the bulbs are too expensive to use them for this purpose.

[2] As a rule species of narcissi and tulips are unsuitable.

---

4. Bulbous and tuberous plants for the rock-garden

In this table all those species have been collected which may be planted in the rock-garden.
This does not imply that they are all specifically mountain plants.

Allium caeruleum
— karataviense
— moly
— neapolitanum
— oreophilum
Anemone blanda
Chionodoxa-species
Colchicum bulbocodium
Corbularia (Narcissus) bulbocodium
Crocus-species
Cyclamen coum
— europaeum
Eranthis-species
Erythronium
Fritillaria imperialis.
Galanthus-species
Ipheion uniflorum
Iris bakeriana
— danfordiae
— histrioides
— reticulata
— tuberosa
Muscari armeniacum
— botryoides

Muscari tubergenianum
Narcissus asturiensis
— cyclamineus
— jonquilla
— nanus
— triandrus
Oxalis-species
Puschkinia scilloides
Scilla-species
Triteleia laxa
Tulipa aucheriana
— batalinii
— celsiana
— clusiana
— eichleri
— greigii
— kaufmanniana
— kolpakowskyana
— linifolia
— tarda
— turkestanica
— urumiensis
— violacea

---

5. Bulbous and tuberous plants for bedding

Bright colours are preferred in flower-beds. Double flowers (tulips!) are very popular for
this purpose. Plants used in beds must have firm stems and preferably be uniform in habit.
Prolonged flowering is also an important characteristic.

Begonia-species
Canna hybrid[1]
Dahlia hybrid (Anemone-flowered)
— — (Collarette)
— — (Mignon)
— — (Topmix)
Hyacinthus hybrid
Muscari armeniacum[2]

Ranunculus asiaticus[3]
Tulipa fosteriana
— group D.L.T.[4]
— — D.E.T.
— — S.E.T.
— — Mendel[5]
— — Triumph

[1] Suitable only for large beds.

98

[2] Usually as a background for other bulbous plants.
[3] Used only occasionally.
[4] Rarely used in Britain.
[5] Very few strains are suitable.

---

6. Bulbous and tuberous plants for window-boxes

There are several disadvantages to placing window-boxes containing spring-flowering plants *in situ* immediately. After all, the bulbs may well be damaged by frost at any time during the winter. This applies particularly to boxes hung or placed on balconies. The best method is, therefore, to plunge the boxes in the garden after having planted the bulbs 8–10 cm (3–4 in.) below the upper edge. In periods of frost the area is covered with straw. Towards spring the boxes are dug up and put in their permanent position where the bulbs are meant to flower. Frost damage is thus avoided and water supply is more reliable. The result will be uniform growth and flowering. Don't forget to make drainage holes in the boxes.

If you have no garden where you can plunge the boxes, they may be stored in a cool cellar, or if necessary they can be kept in peat in large chests on the balcony.

In principle many of the species mentioned in this book can be used in window-boxes[1], but the most suitable are:

Begonia-species
Crocus vernus hybrids
Dahlia hybrid (Mignon)
— — (Topmix)
Hyacinthus hybrid
Muscari armeniacum
Narcissus cyclamineus[2]

Tulipa greigii
— group double early
— — single early
— — Triumph
— kaufmanniana
— praestans

[1] There is nothing to prevent you from growing small iris species, allium, Glory of the snow, puschkinia, oxalis, etc. in pots or boxes on your balcony.

[2] Other narcissi, such as trumpet daffodils, are sometimes used by municipal parks and gardens departments in large street containers, etc.

7. Bulbs and tubers for forcing indoors

Although this subject is really outside the scope of this book, we should nevertheless like to give it some attention.

In October we fill a number of pots with fine garden soil and plant the bulbs with their tips just above the rim of the pot (tulips, hyacinths and narcissi). Smaller bulbs may be planted with their tips level or just below the rim. The distance between the bulbs can be small, e.g. 2 cm ($\frac{3}{4}$ in.). The pots are then buried in the garden; in the case of tulips, narcissi and hyacinths this is done at a depth of $\pm$ 15 cm (that is, a layer of 15 cm (6 in.) deep above the pots). Pots containing the smaller fry are covered with a depth of only about 5 cm (2 in.). At the onset of frost we cover the spot where the pots have been buried with a good layer of straw, bracken or leaves.

If you do not have a garden, the pots may be buried in a large box filled with, for instance, a mixture of garden soil and peat. The box can be put on a balcony, but special care should be taken to protect it against frost. Watering also needs care. In the last resort the potted bulbs may even be placed in a cool cellar, preferably at a temperature of $\pm$ 10° C (50° F). Make sure the soil is kept sufficiently damp.

Apart from the species listed below there are a number of others which can be brought to flower indoors. For instance, there are special canna strains for indoor use, and Begonia multiflora flourishes on a window-sill. Zephyranthes, too, feels quite at home in the living-room. The following are suitable for forcing:

Chionodoxa-species[1]
Colchicum autumnale[2]
Crocus chrysanthus[1]
— flavus 'Luteus'[1]
— vernus hybrids[1]
Galanthus nivalis[3]
Hyacinthus hybrid[4]
Iris danfordiae[1]
— histrioides[1]
— reticulata[1]
Muscari armeniacum[1]
— botryoides[1]

Muscari tubergenianum[1]
Narcissus-species[5]
Oxalis adenophylla[1]
Puschkinia scilloides[1]
Sauromatum venosum[6]
Scilla bifolia[1]
— sibirica[1]
— tubergeniana[1]
Tulipa group D.E.T.[7]
— group S.E.T.
— group Triumph
— kaufmanniana

[1] These species can be brought indoors four to six weeks before they normally flower. However, for grape hyacinths the correct time is mid-February, whereas oxalis, for instance, prefers to come 'into the warm' in early March. The temperature should not be too high; this applies to practically all species. For most of them a temperature of $\pm$ 12° C (54° F) is ideal. Make sure they get enough water.

[2] The dry bulb is placed on the window-sill in August; after some time the flowers will come out.

[3] Place indoors in January, as cool as possible. Requires a fair amount of water.

[4] Do not bring these indoors until the flowers have emerged from the bulbs — this can be judged from the shape of the shoot. Room temperature 20° C (68° F).

[5] Around mid-January the flowerbuds can be seen between the leaves. This is the time to bring them indoors. Preferred room temperature is $\pm$ 16° C (60° F).

[6] Will flower on the window-sill in spring, but has a disagreeable smell.

[7] Other tulip groups may be used as well. They sometimes grow too tall for indoor use. As soon as the buds can be felt in the shoot they may be brought indoors. By then the shoot is often 6–8 cm (2½–3½ in.) tall, but this is not a decisive factor. Temperature should preferably not exceed 18° C (65° F).

---

8. Bulbs, corms and tubers in the flora of Britain

In recent years interest in our indigenous flora has greatly increased. Wild plants are given their rightful chance in the garden and are no longer carelessly discarded as 'weeds'. There are even enthusiasts who plant their entire garden with native trees, shrubs, perennials and annuals. Among the plants growing wild in this country there are, of course, a number of bulbous and tuberous ones. In some cases they have not always been there. Sometimes they have 'escaped' from places where they have been cultivated for years. When these 'guest plants' have no disturbing effect on the vegetation already there, they may well be counted among the wild flora, especially if they maintain themselves without human help. If you are not too much of a purist you might plant certain other species as well, such as the winter aconite.

Allium ursinum
Anemone nemorosa
Colchicum autumnale
Convallaria majalis
Corydalis cava
– solida
Fritillaria meleagris
Galanthus nivalis
Leucojum aestivum
– vernum

Muscari racemosum
Narcissus pseudonarcissus[1]
Ornithogalum nutans
– umbellatum
Polygonatum odoratum
– multiflorum
Scilla non-scripta
Tulipa silvestris[2]

[1] This wild daffodil, which, as far as I know, is not in cultivation, maintains itself in some places for dozens of years. Some botanists speak of 'flora-falsification', but this seems too harsh a term for people who sow or plant certain species in the wild which are probably, or certainly, not native to this country.

[2] This wild tulip is not mentioned anywhere else in this book. According to the Clapham, Tutin and Warburg *Flora of the British Isles* its occurrence in England is probably due to the fact that it naturalised after having been cultivated in earlier centuries. The flowers are yellow, greenish outside.

---

9. Bulbs which must be kept dry and frost-free in winter

A limited number of bulbous and tuberous plants are unable to survive our winters out of doors. They suffer from frost, and especially from damp. Apart from those mentioned below this applies also, for instance, to the freesia, but in any case these cannot be brought to flower a second time unless they are treated at a certain temperature. It is therefore useless to store them yourself.

Bulbs and tubers which do not tolerate cold or damp are lifted in October. Make sure they are perfectly dry before storing them, otherwise they will grow mouldy. The ones in the list which follow may survive outdoors in gardens in the south-west, in really warm, sheltered conditions.

Acidanthera bicolor[1]	Gladiolus hybrid — 'Gandavensis'[3]
Anemone coronaria[2]	Ornithogalum thyrsoides[1]
Begonia-species[3]	Oxalis deppei[3]
Canna hybrid[1]	Ranunculus asiaticus[4]
Dahlia hybrid[3]	Sauromatum venosum[3]
Eucomis bicolor[3]	Sprekelia formosissima[1]
Galtonia candicans[3]	Tigridia pavonia[3]

[1] Should be stored in a fairly warm place, $\pm$ 15–20° C (59–68° F).
[2] Should be stored in a cool place: quality deteriorates rapidly.
[3] May be stored in a cool place.
[4] The Turkish ranunculus is an exception.

---

10. Bulbs and tubers planted in autumn

The planting season of the different species varies between October and December 15. For the exact planting time see the relevant chapter.

Allium-species	Gladiolus hybrid 'Colvillei'
Anemone blanda	— nanus
— nemorosa	Hyacinthus hybrid
— pavonina	Ipheion uniflorum
Camassia-species	Iris-species
Chionodoxa-species	Ixia hybrid
Colchicum autumnale[1]	Ixiolirion pallasii
— bulbocodium	Leucojum-species
Convallaria majalis[2]	Lilium candidum
Corbularia (Narcissus) bulbocodium	— hollandicum
Corydalis-species	— pumilum
Crocus-species	Muscari-species
Cyclamen-species	Narcissus-species
Eranthis-species	Ornithogalum nutans
Eremurus x shelford	— umbellatum
Erythronium-species	Oxalis adenophylla
Fritillaria-species	Polygonatum-species[2]
Galanthus-species	Puschkinia scilloides
Gladiolus byzantinus	Ranunculus asiaticus[4]

Scilla-species
Sparaxis tricolor

Triteleia laxa
Tulipa-species

[1] Planted in July.
[2] Can also be planted in spring.
[3] Autumn-flowering species are planted in July.
[4] Only the Turkish ranunculus is planted in the autumn.

---

11. Bulbs and tubers planted in spring

Some species, for instance canna, begonia and dahlia cuttings, cannot be planted until the end of May—early June. Others, such as, for instance, acidanthera and galtonia, are entrusted to the soil in April.

Acidanthera bicolor
Anemone coronaria
Begonia
Bletilla striata
Canna hybrid
Crinum powellii
Crocosmia crocosmiiflora
Dahlia hybrid
Eucomis bicolor
Freesia hybrid
Galtonia candicans
Gladiolus hybrid — 'Gandavensis'
Lilium auratum

Lilium henryi
— hybrid 'Midcentury'
— martagon
— regale
— speciosum
— tigrinum
Ornithogalum thyrsoides
Oxalis deppei
Ranunculus asiaticus[1]
Sauromatum venosum
Sprekelia formosissima
Tigridia pavonia
Zephyranthes candida

[1] Turkish ranunculi are planted in the autumn.

12. Bulbous plants flowering in January, February and March

The flowering season of these very early plants naturally depends greatly on weather conditions. In some years it may freeze as late as March, which of course delays flowering. In all cases the earliest possible flowering season in the most favourable weather conditions has been mentioned.

Anemone blanda
— nemorosa
Chionodoxa-species
Colchicum bulbocodium
Corydalis solida
Crocus chrysanthus
— etruscus
— flavus 'Luteus'
— sieberi
— tomasinianus
— vernus hybrids
Cyclamen coum
Eranthis-species
Erythronium dens-canis
Galanthus-species

Iris bakeriana
— bucharica
— danfordiae
— histrioides
— magnifica
— reticulata
Leucojum vernum
Narcissus cyclamineus
Puschkinia scilloides
Scilla bifolia
— sibirica
— tubergeniana
Tulipa kaufmanniana
— violacea

---

13. Bulbous plants flowering in April and May

Here, too, the weather may affect the flowering season, although to a lesser extent. There are, moreover, several species listed in table 12 which may still flower profusely in April. In any case a great many bulbous and tuberous plants are at their best in these two months.

Allium karataviense
— moly[1]
— triquetrum
— ursinum
Anemone pavonina
Camassia cusickii
— leichtlinii
Convallaria majalis
Corbularia (Narcissus) bulbocodium
Corydalis cava
Erythronium revolutum
— tuolumnense
Fritillaria imperialis
— meleagris
Ipheion uniflorum

Iris hybrid (Iris hollandica)
— hoogiana
— tuberosa
Leucojum aestivum
Muscari-species
Narcissus-species[2]
Ornithogalum nutans
— umbellatum
Oxalis adenophylla
Polygonatum-species
Sauromatum venosum
Scilla hispanica
— non-scripta
— pratensis

[1] Usually this yellow allium does not flower until the beginning of June. If the bulbs have been left *in situ*, they may flower in late May.

[2] Some Narcissus cyclamineus strains may easily flower in late February—early March. In favourable weather conditions a number of trumpet daffodils or large-cupped narcissi, which have been left undisturbed for years — for instance, against a south-facing wall — may flower at the end of March.

[3] Apart from the two species mentioned in table 12.

---

14. Bulbous and tuberous plants flowering in June, July, August and September

These are a rather neglected group, for with the exception of dahlia and begonia they are not over-popular. Even lilies, which are, after all, among the most beautiful flowers, are found only too rarely in our gardens.

Acidanthera bicolor
Allium caeruleum
— giganteum
— neapolitanum
— oreophilum
— sphaerocephalum
Anemone coronaria
Begonia-species
Camassia quamash
Canna hybrid
Colchicum autumnale
Crinum powellii
Crocosmia crocosmiiflora
Crocus kotschyanus
— speciosus
Cyclamen europaeum
Dahlia hybrid
Eremurus x shelford[1]
Eucomis bicolor

Freesia hybrid
Galtonia candicans
Gladiolus byzantinus
— hybr. — 'Colvillei'[2]
— hybr. — 'Gandavensis'
— nanus[2]
Iris xiphioides
Ixia hybrid
Ixiolirion pallasii
Lilium-species
Ornithogalum thyrsoides
Oxalis deppei
Ranunculus asiaticus[3]
Sparaxis tricolor
Sprekelia formosissima
Tigridia pavonia
Triteleia laxa
Zephyranthes candida

[1] Some eremurus species, such as E. himalaicus and E. robustus may flower as early as May.
[2] Flowering in the second half of May is not impossible.
[3] Turkish ranunculi flower as early as the end of April—beginning of May.

WELL WORTH A VISIT

Show gardens, events and exhibitions in the bulb world

In a recent survey conducted by the Royal Horticultural Society with regard to the most popular plants grown by members in their gardens, it was found that bulbs topped the list, being grown by 95 per cent of the members — lawns and roses took second place.

Half of the world's daffodil acreage is found in England, and more of these bulbs are grown in Lincolnshire than in the whole of Holland, but Holland is the home of the tulip, and that country exported 1,200 million tulip bulbs in 1972.

If you would like to see displays of all kinds of bulbs in bloom, the following is a list of gardens, flower parades and nurseries which will provide all the spectacle and information you can absorb, both in England and in Holland, Europe's leading bulb-growing countries.

SPRINGFIELDS

The centre of the bulb industry in Britain is Lincolnshire and, as the industry has been expanding rapidly during the last 15 years, it was decided that there was a need for some kind of bulb display garden which would give both the private gardener and the trade a source of sound information and advice on bulbs with regard to appearance, cultivation, quality, varieties and so on. Accordingly a site was decided on, and work was begun to convert 20 acres of flat, bare Fenland into the beautiful garden which exists today. It was opened in 1966, and contains 30,000 shrubs and trees, a lake, lawns, a model garden, a 'variety' glasshouse, an 'indoor garden' glasshouse and an aviary of exotic birds, besides a tremendous collection of bulb species, cultivars and hybrids.

Bulbs can be ordered at the Garden, and there is an information bureau giving cultural advice on bulb growing. Springfields is open daily from the beginning of April to the third week in May; early in the season the display in the vast greenhouses is at its best while outdoor bulbs are not yet in flower. The garden is situated one mile east of Spalding on the A151 Spalding–Holbeach road. Further information can be obtained from: Springfields, Spalding, Lincs (Tel. 0775–4843).

SPALDING FLOWER PARADE (and other flower festivals)

This Flower Parade is internationally famous; it takes place in about the second week of May every year, and contains more than 40 floats decorated with a total of between six and eight million tulip heads. Together with massed bands and the Tulip Queen, the Parade provides a mile-long floral spectacle covering a route of four miles in and around Spalding. The floats are also on view for two or three days at a special stationery exhibition both before and after the Parade.

In addition, there are Flower Festivals in the villages around Spalding at the same time, and the thousands of acres of bulb fields contain daffodils and tulips, a sight in themselves not to be missed.

For further information as to dates, times and prices of admission, enquiries should be made to the Flower Parade, c/o Springfields, Spalding.

KEUKENHOF, Holland
Nearest railway station, Lisse

Open daily between 8 a.m. and half an hour after sunset from the end of March to the second half of May.

The Keukenhof can be reached from Leyden and Haarlem by buses run by the N.Z.H., which stop at the entrance. Combined rail–bus–entrance tickets may be obtained from railway stations throughout Holland. For motorists the roads to the Keukenhof are clearly signposted. There is plenty of parking space.

The Keukenhof, at one time the Countess Jacoba van Beieren's hunting estate, occupies a gently sloping terrain. The park, which covers approximately 28 hectares (70 acres), contains magnificent trees. No fewer than 4–5 million bulbs are planted in this natural setting every year. The greenhouses, where the most fantastically shaped and coloured tulips are displayed, cover an area of 5,000 square metres (yards).

In 1972 650,000 people visited this unique bulb event, known also for its sculpture.

REFUGIUM BOTANICUM
Haarlem, Holland

Without disrespect for other bulb growers, Messrs. van Tubergen must be mentioned for their 'Refugium Botanicum' – the last refuge for (lovers of) unusual bulbous plants. The firm is practically the only one in the Netherlands to market all kinds of rare bulbous and tuberous products. On request they will send a comprehensive price-list. The nurseries can be visited by appointment (Tel. 023–316750). The address is Kweekery Zwanenburg, P.O. Box 116, Haarlem.

BULB ROUTE A.N.W.B., Holland

In the period from the second half of March to the second half of May a tour through the flowering bulb-fields is well worth the trouble. The A.N.W.B. (Automobile Association) has planned a special route in the region between Haarlem and Wassenaar, indicated by unusual six-sided signposts. To make the trip more enjoyable you are advised to go on a weekday, for on 'Bulb-Sundays' the traffic is unbelievable.

Bulbs are grown on a large scale also in the region called the 'Streek', which lies between Enkhuizen, Grootebroek and Andijk in the province of North Holland. To see the bulb-fields here you can follow the so-called 'Koggenroute'.

In addition the V.V.V. (Tourist Association) has set out routes in the Wieringermeer and the 'Streek', the so-called 'Holland's Glory' route.

If you don't want to be tied by any special route, you could follow the coast road between Castricum and Bergen, or make a tour in the Anna–Paulownapolder and Breezland, south-east of Den Helder.

FLOWER CORSO, Holland

The well-known bulb pageant in the bulb region usually takes place on the last Saturday in April. On that occasion more than 20 floats travel between Haarlem and Sassenheim, a distance of 25 km (16 miles). The procession usually leaves Haarlem at around 10 a.m. It reaches Bennebroek at 12.15 and halts here until 2 p.m. It arrives in Hillegom and Lisse at 2.40 and 3.35 respectively, and as a rule reaches the terminal point in Sassenheim at around 5 p.m. Many of the floats stay here on exhibition over the weekend.

The floats can be seen beforehand on Friday between 11 a.m. and midnight in the auction halls of HoBaHo and H.B.G. in Lisse; there is an entrance fee.

As the time of departure, the route and the entrance fees are subject to alteration, you are advised to telephone the V.V.V. in Lisse beforehand.

LILIADE
Akkersloot, Holland

This can be reached by bus from the railway stations in Assendelft and Alkmaar; at the time of the exhibition there is a regular ferry service. As a rule this unique show takes place in the first week of July. The exact date depends on the preceding growing period and may therefore vary somewhat.

No fewer than 120–140 different lily species are shown here. Sometimes the lily-show is combined with exhibitions of other flowers, e.g. sweetpeas or fuchsias.

INDEX